Victorian DRESS
IN PHOTOGRAPHS

Victorian DRESS

IN PHOTOGRAPHS

Madeleine Ginsburg

B. T. BATSFORD LTD. LONDON

*Dedicated to R. S. who taught me how to see
and to the late C. G.-S. who showed me where to look*

*Dedicated to R. S. who taught me how to see
and to the late C. G.-S. who showed me where to look*

© Madeleine Ginsburg 1982
First published 1982

This paperback edition published 1988

ISBN 0 7134 6038 5

Typeset by Keyspools Ltd, Golborne, Lancashire,
and printed in Great Britain by
The Bath Press, Bath, Avon

for the publishers
B. T. Batsford Ltd.
4 Fitzhardinge Street
London W1H 0AH

Contents

Introduction

The photographs have been chosen to illustrate the range of clothing and the sequence of fashion changes in Britain throughout the Victorian era. They have been arranged in four groups: fashionable dress for women and for men from 1841 to 1900, children's clothes and occupational and regional working dress. Those that are dated precisely because there is internal evidence are noted so, while others are dated by association. Altogether there are 253 images providing the student of modes and manners and the fashion and costume designer with a picture of the past more complete in itself than that from any other source. Fashion plates acquire humanity when clothes are seen to be worn by those who have chosen them for their smartness, suitability or function, with accessories to suit. Diagrams of cut assume new meaning when the garments can be viewed in the round and on real people.

For the collector of photographs the series may serve another purpose by helping to date or place items which have lost their context or identification. The pace of fashion may change through the decades, from place to place and from wearer to wearer, but within all these variations a verifiable sequence remains into which most photographs of the dressed (and even some of the undressed), the dowdy as well as the smart, can be fitted with almost the same accuracy that we use when assessing our contemporaries. The only rule to follow is that the outfit cannot be earlier than the earliest datable feature that it displays. Indeed the photograph collector has as much to gain in collecting fashion plates as the fashion student has in amassing photographs.

The commentaries in the appendix summarise the developments within each period and so far as possible I have done this through sources contemporary with the photographs, thus letting people similar to those shown tell the story in their own words.

Madeleine Ginsburg   *London 1982*

Acknowledgment

My thanks are due to my family for their sometimes amused, often exasperated but always appreciated support during a period which seemed to them unnecessarily prolonged; and as always to H.A., L.G. and L.B.G. and D.L. for practical assistance far beyond the bonds of love and friendship.

All the photographic collections provided good humoured help to a permanent beginner in their subject, renewing my enthusiasm for the project. I hope this book will go a small way to repay my debt for the inroads I made on their time, patience and expertise.

In particular my grateful thanks to Brian Coe of the Kodak Museum, also to Don Cookson, who helped him to share the added burden of the associated exhibition. In addition I was greatly helped by Mark Haworth-Booth of the Victoria and Albert Museum, Bernard Howarth-Loomes and by John Ward of the Science Museum. Most useful advice came from Peter Castle, Celestine Dars, Colin Ford, Giles Gordon, Wendy Hefford, Professor Margaret Harker, Tina Levey, Valerie Lloyd, Sara Stevenson, Dr Thomas and Pat White.

Help well beyond mere loan of photographs was given me by Kate Lloyd, Alex Noble, the Hon. Mrs Pepys, 'Peter Robinson', Gerald Lund, E.J. Sidery and the staffs of the Gallery of English Costume, Manchester, the Museum of English Rural Life, Reading, the National Portrait Gallery, the Public Record Office, the Theatre Museum and Trinity College Cambridge.

Without today's photographers a project of this kind would not have been practicable; I would like to record my appreciation of the skill and patience of the late Mr Bishop, of Jonathan Rosen and of Peter MacDonald and his colleagues in the Photography Studio of the Victoria and Albert Museum.

Finally, thanks to Sam Carr, whose idea this was in the first place, Belinda Baker who helped to cope, Gillian Gibbins who did the design and to all members of the public and the costume specialists whose constant enquiries about the appearance and the background of people in the past provided me with the continuous stimulus which got me through to the end.

The author and the publishers are grateful to the following for their permission to reproduce the photographs used in this book: Aberdeen Public Library (253); BBC Hulton Picture Library (97); Barnardo's Photo Library (148); Birmingham Public Library (123, 124, 210); Boyer Collection, Sandwich (46, 191, 222–224, 227, 228); Gallery of English Costume, Platt Hall, Manchester (84, 151, 231); Gernsheim Collection, Humanities Research Centre, University of Texas at Austin (141); Kodak Museum (59, 70, 103, 119, 125, 126, 130, 131, 157, 160, 161, 182, 186, 190, 238, 239); Bernard Howarth-Loomes Collection (26, 36–38, 135, 211); Manchester Public Library (240); Marylebone Cricket Club (187); Museum of English Rural Life, Reading (226); National Portrait Gallery (12, 47, 48, 55, 112, 113, 137, 142, 180, 198, 208, 246); National Trust, Lacock Abbey (165, 229); The Hon. Mrs Pepys (163); Peter Robinson (52–54); Public Record Office (69, 73, 204–207); Rothman Collection (237, 251); Royal Photographic Society (220); Science Museum (2, 4–10, 15–17, 20, 132, 133, 167, 168, 171, 172, 174, 218); Scottish National Portrait Gallery (11, 13, 14); The Theatre Museum (28, 29, 39–42, 56, 57, 61, 72, 74, 76, 78–80, 85, 90, 94, 95, 100, 101, 110, 118, 121, 127–129, 155, 175, 177, 181, 183, 184, 188, 196, 197, 199–201, 214, 215, 232); Trinity College, Cambridge (212, 213, 219, 221, 233, 236); Victoria and Albert Museum (3, 18, 19, 22, 24, 25, 30–34, 43–45, 49–51, 58, 63–68, 71, 75, 77, 82, 83, 86–88, 89, 91–93, 96, 98, 99, 102, 104–109, 111, 117, 134, 136, 138–140, 143–147, 149, 150, 152, 153, 156, 158, 159, 162, 164, 166, 170, 173, 176, 178, 179, 185, 189, 192, 194, 195, 202, 203, 209, 225, 234, 235, 242–245, 247–249, 250, 252); Reece Winstone (230); Nos. 1, 21, 23, 27, 35, 60, 62, 120, 122, 133, 169, 216 and 217 are from the publishers' collection. Nos. 115, 116, 162 and 193 are from private collections.

7

Clothes in Camera

One of the aims of the pioneer photographers of Victorian Britain was to compile a pictorial record of the age in which they lived. It was a privilege and a duty for they were gratefully conscious that with the invention of the camera they had become the first generation to have the means of showing the present to the future without alteration or amendment. Clothes and personal appearance came within their terms of reference and, aware that posterity might find them somewhat bizarre, they looked to photography to redress the balance. The ladies in particular might need some reassessment, for as A. R. Wallace somewhat chauvinistically noted in 1889, in the pictorial record 'as say represented by Frith and Dumaurier', two decades had so altered their appearance that a future historian might 'ascribe it to the introduction of some foreign race', a mistaken conclusion which might be avoided by the use of the photograph so that 'our descendants in the middle of the twentieth century will be able to see how much and what kind of change really did occur from age to age'.

The record is rich, the product of most of the great names in Victorian photography. It is copious and it is varied, providing a dated or datable record of six decades of fashion changes for the smart and the dowdy, the town and the country dweller. It is also accessible, in museum, in picture book and in old family album; yet Wallace's advice has been rarely followed. It is now over a century since that not-too-successful Victorian engraver, Charles Landseer, described photography as 'Foe-to-graphic art', but in the study of the history of dress the engraved fashion plate still reigns supreme and most people are only too willingly seduced by its highly coloured and somewhat meretricious appeal, and rarely deterred by its limited range.

Not that the fashion plate is without its uses even to the specialist collector of photographs, for, where internal evidence is lacking, the clothes and by implication the wearer can be dated by analysis of an established and precisely datable sequence of the style of dress, using the principle that no photograph can be earlier than the earliest fashion feature seen within it. It is a debt which photography repays with interest for to the student of modes and manners as well as to the fashion and costume designer, it provides a picture of the past more complete than that available from any other sources and is an essential complement to them. Here are clothes which have moved from the drawing board into a real-life world, have been made up, accessoried and finally worn by ordinary human beings who not only lived but must, incredible as the fashionable constrictions and restrictions seem to our appalled twentieth-century eyes, have both moved and breathed!

So why has photography been neglected as a source for the history of dress, yielding but one specialised book? Alison Gernsheim's *Fashion and Reality* was published almost 20 years ago and has long been out of print. Possibly the main reason is the overwhelming quantity of material which survives, despite negatives and prints being so fragile. The pioneers of the new technique regarded the very real technical limitations as a challenge rather than as a barrier and it is difficult for the student to avoid being buried by the sheer weight of the evidence. Fortunately publications such as the Royal Photographic Society's *Directory of British Photographic Collections* provide at least initial guidance and there is a steadily increasing stream of monographs on both photographers and techniques, as well as catalogues of collections, public, private and commercial. Unfortunately Victorian prints do not always take kindly to modern commercial reproduction and for this reason I have concentrated on examples in public collections where the originals can be consulted.

But the images are only part of the story and the identity of the sitters, and when and where they sat for their photographs are often matters of conjecture, though very relevant considerations. Self-conscious as the early photographers were about their importance as recorders of the new age they were not always as quick to note the circumstances as they were to record the scene, so that identifying their sitters and placing them in their social and geographical context often poses problems which should be solved before those interested in fashion or its more workaday version, dress, can use the source or fully appreciate the significance. If anything the lack of documentation is even greater for the professional than for the amateur. If photographic archives are prone to separation and depredation how much more so are the negative guard books, those vast and usually crumbling tomes containing an apparently cryptic series of numbers, names and dates which are the commercial lifeline of the professional photographer – his most important business record – and our most important source.

In any case the role of objective recorder did not content the early photographers for long. They had no sooner mastered their techniques than they began to manipulate them and if the camera could not lie it could certainly be made to prevaricate. Despite the impeccably Victorian background of the concept, truth was not always beauty either to photographers or to their sitters and these last were sometimes not above adding their own element of distortion to the record. Personal inscriptions are often misleading either by default or error or by design. It is by no means only the professional beauty who through forgetfulness or perhaps for economy, sends old and usually more flattering photographs to new friends.

Men and women alike, the sitters add their own concept of truth and quota of illusion to confuse the observer. They prefer to confront the cold gaze of posterity in clothes which are suitable rather than smart, following clothing conventions applicable to their class and occupation which may blur or distort the accepted fashion-plate image. The respectable tend to obey the 'golden rule', as set out in the *Ladies' Treasury* in 1858, that 'propriety must be studied before fashion', and that 'no fashion should be adopted until it becomes more singular not to adopt than to follow it'. This process observed among the urban middle class might delay acceptance of a style at least for a year or two, and the time lag increases further down the social scale and in more remote areas. It is a factor which must be taken into account when studying photographs. A similarly conservative attitude was recommended to men, for according to the *Habits of Good Society*, 'after the turning point of life, a man should eschew the changes of fashion in his own attire'. Both comments were written midway through the century but in general hold good throughout. The principle applied even more strongly to hairstyles and far too many subjects, especially the middle-aged, remain faithful to the hairdressing which was fashionable in their prime, Alexandra, Princess of Wales quite as much as any anonymous great-grandmother. It is an ineradicable human characteristic quite as common today as it ever was in the nineteenth century, and a particularly unfortunate one in the portrait photograph where the coiffure can be the most visible fashion feature. In the economical head-and-shoulders view it is often the least useful point of reference, except in so far as it suggests the earliest date for a likeness.

Fortunately the stage flourished by observing the converse of this advice and actors were well aware that, as the *Ladies' Treasury* warned, 'any change of costume excites attention; and this attention is unavoidably transferred from the dress to the wearer whose . . . beauties are thus brought predominantly into notice'. It is through actors and actresses that we can best appreciate high-style Victorian dress.

Even though things are not necessarily quite what they seem, the photograph still retains its historical reality; viewed analytically and with care it transcends accidental or conscious distortion to show us today people and their clothes as they really were. The desire to copy an image is as old as art itself, yet photography as we know it was the child of the nineteenth century. The earliest attempt to apply the principles of optics to ease the chore of representation, the *camera obscura*, was certainly in use by the sixteenth century but the problem of perpetuating the image was chemical. It was only solved in 1826 when Nicèphore Niépce (1765–1833) managed to focus and fix permanently onto a chemically treated pewter plate the scene outside his Châlons window. The practical process which evolved was named after his collaborator Louis Jacques Mandé Daguerre (1787–1854), scene painter and stage illusionist, who refined and improved it. Its range was restricted to the inanimate and portraits could not be attempted until a way had been found to reduce the exposure time from hours to minutes and it was not until 1841 that the camera could record anyone who had the fortitude to spend two minutes completely immobile in bright sunshine. Daguerre announced his discovery to the French Académie des Sciences in 1839 and with a blaze of world-wide publicity the daguerreotype was born, the polished metal plate whose shadow image was to provide a most precise picture of the predominantly well-to-do from the 1840s to the mid-1850s.

The first professional English portrait daguerreotypist was Richard Beard (1801–85), coal merchant turned cameraman, who opened his roof-top studio in the London Polytechnic building in 1841 using an American patent camera with an amended sensitizing method to accelerate the exposure. The famous queued to toil up the stairs into the circular studio suffused with mysterious shaded blue daylight which filtered down onto a central revolving chair well provided with supportive straps and stays, avid to see whether, in the words of S. L. Blanchard's 'New school of portrait painting' (published in the Cruikshank Omnibus 1842), their 'image reversed will minutely appear, so delicate, forcible, brilliant and clear'. Beard was the first Englishman to see the commercial potential of Daguerre's invention but he was almost immediately rivalled and then surpassed by Antoine François Jean Claudet (1797–1867), the first English licensee of Daguerre's patent, as well as by the American John Jabez Mayall (1810–1901), an early specialist in group portraiture, and William Edward Kilburn (fl. 1850s) to mention only the most notable London practitioners. Knowledge of the techniques spread rapidly and there were soon licensed studios in most of the main provincial towns as well as innumerable unrecorded and unlicensed pirate enterprises.

Good daguerreotypes seem rare in England and their range is limited, partly because they were so expensive. The process, free to the rest of the world, in England was protected by patent. Claudet charged two guineas for a full-length portrait, one guinea for a half-length and five shillings for colouring, at a time when a fair wage for a skilled man was about £3 per week and only half that amount for the average worker, so that on the whole it was a process confined to the upper and prosperous middle classes. The daguerreotype was also fragile and since it was technically a negative viewed as a positive, each image was individual and could not be multiplied. Nevertheless sufficient

remain to suggest that the sitters were not disappointed, for they have an admirable clarity.

Daguerre was not the only one concerned with the problem of perpetuating an image. At the same time William Henry Fox Talbot (1800–77), a Wiltshire country gentleman with artistic interests and a scientific bent, working quite independently, had discovered how to fix a shadow image onto paper, which he called a 'photogenic drawing'. By 1840 he too had reduced the exposure time necessary from an hour to between one and three minutes, depending on light conditions. An additional advantage of his method was that multiple copies could be made from the same negative image. This calotype, or as it is sometimes called, talbotype, was patented in 1841. It was the first negative process and the origin of the photograph as we know it today.

Fox Talbot's first portrait, of his wife Constance, was taken in October 1840. During the next decade he made many photographs of his family, friends and his house staff at Lacock Abbey, Wiltshire – where a converted barn now houses the Fox Talbot Museum – and here, as in the Science Museum photographic collection, they can still be seen. They are particularly valuable because they include full-length, relaxed, informal, upper middle class family groups as well as a fair range of artisans and agricultural labourers.

Less well-known but just as useful as sources and possibly even better documented are the calotypes taken by Fox Talbot's Welsh cousin and correspondent John Dillwyn Llewellyn (1810–82) which his daughter Thereza dated and mentioned in her diary.

To explain and publicise his process Fox Talbot produced and had published a set of plates, with explanatory text, The Pencil of Nature, 1844–46. Plate V, 'The Ladder', intended as a study in composition, provides incidental comment on men's clothes of the period. It almost deserves a subtitle, borrowed from Disraeli: the Privileged and the People. The gentleman (a rare invaluable back view this), both the dress and pose an echo of an 1840 fashion plate by B. Read, is constricted in wasp-waisted coat and straight-cut trousers of an almost Regency outline, as formal and reactionary in his dress as the labourer in practical loose-cut trousers and easy-fitting waistcoat is forward looking. It is an apt illustration of costume historian Sir James Laver's thesis that in working, informal and sports clothes the seeds of future sartorial development are to be found. In his Plate I, lace of a fashionable kind is used to illustrate the scope of the negative while a photograph of serried ranks of the caps and bonnets of the ladies of the family, used as an illustration in *The Art Union*, demonstrates the camera's time-saving ability to record a multiplicity of objects.

Despite its convenience the calotype was less popular with the first generation of English professional photographers than the daguerreotype. The licence fee Fox Talbot demanded was inhibitingly high and clients preferred the linear precision of the daguerreotype to the textural quality of the paper print.

It was in Scotland, where Fox Talbot's patent did not apply, that the best known examples of the calotype portrait were to be found. David Octavius Hill (1802–70), the energetic secretary of the Royal Scottish Academy as well as an artist of national repute, had decided to paint a group portrait of the signing in May 1843 of the Deed of Demission, the foundation charter of the Free Church of Scotland. It was a complex task, posing a number of daunting practical problems, for 300 ministers were involved as well as a number of other dignitaries. Fortunately Hill and Fox Talbot had a mutual friend, Sir David Brewster, who both appreciated the labour-saving potential of this new technique of photography and could recommend a trained practitioner, young Robert Adamson (1821–48), thus bringing about a partnership which was to be one of the most significant in the history of photography.

By the autumn of 1843, Hill and Adamson had taken 301 of the portraits they required as models, but despite this progress the painting was not to be finished for another 20 years. Two hundred calotypes of the 450 likenesses in it are known to exist and provide an excellent visual record of the dress and appearance of a large cross-section of the guardians of the Scottish conscience. The clergymen can be recognised by their white bands or cravats, the conventional badge of their calling, but the laymen are more varied in their clothing and accessories. In the group portrait, not completed until 1861, the 'spoon' bonnets of the ladies, obviously the latest additions, contrast uneasily with the predominantly 1840-type clothing of the majority and as a whole it confirms Hill's talents as a photographer rather than a painter.

Hill and Adamson continued to expand their activities, specialising in group portraits such as that of the British Association of Science in 1844, and between 1843 and 1847 nearly every notable visitor to Scotland, as well as numerous friends and relations, patronised their studio on the west terrace of Rock House, Hill's home in Edinburgh. The intellectuals and academics form a distinct group with sartorial idiosyncracies more illustrative of individual philosophies than conventional contemporary modes, but the majority blend more or less indistinguishably with Fox Talbot's subjects, though the Lacock Abbey groups tend to be easy and domestic while most of the Edinburgh sitters are more self-conscious and formal. The analogy between the poses of the latter and those of fashion plates has been pointed out by Sir Roy Strong in the introduction to the National Portrait Gallery's *Hill and Adamson Album*.

Taken together the two sets of subjects, Scottish and English, form a useful group of typical upper middle and professional class early Victorians. For the first time in history we can see a generation as they saw themselves. The men, on formal occasions, are constricted in high-cut collars rising from sloping shoulder lines and tight pantaloons, but informally easy in loose-cut tweeds. The ladies, their hair centre-parted with mathematical precision, wear dresses with sloping shoulder lines, tight low-waisted bodices and skirts full but less bouffant or ornate than in the fashion plates.

Naturally there is a Scottish bias. There are some sitters who wear tartan or Highland dress but the best known are the fisher-folk from Newhaven outside Edinburgh taken in 1845, probably as part of a local vicar's fund-raising appeal for new boats. This was the first appearance of the photogenic peasant, an idea to be developed in the 1860s by Francis Frith, the picture postcard pioneer. The picturesque garb with its links with eighteenth-century rural modes has been the subject of intensive study by the Costume Society of Scotland.

By the middle of the nineteenth century photography was becoming accepted and beginning to lose its novelty if not its mystique, and the record begins to accumulate. The 1851 Great Exhibition included an important photographic section, an international shop-window for processes and techniques, somewhat depressing for the English who found themselves outpaced in almost every field, with the Americans producing the best daguerreotypes and the French the best paper prints. Nevertheless, within the British Isles the numbers of professionals continued to rise dramatically from 51 in 1851 to 2,879 in 1861 and they were now to be found in almost every town in the Kingdom.

In part, this was due to the remission of the calotype patent in 1854 and the supplanting of the daguerreotype by the glass negative with positive copies. The whole process was improved and simplified by a series of new developments. Frederick Scott Archer (1813–57) introduced his much faster and more sensitive wet plate or collodion process in 1851 and Louis Désiré Blanquart Evrard his improved albumen printing paper in 1850 while in his Lille printing establishment he pioneered the mass production of albumen-coated prints. It was now possible to produce multiple cheap, copy-prints, repeats of photographs of almost daguerreotype sharpness yet taken with comparatively short exposure.

The formal seal of acceptance of the photograph was in 1854 with the founding of the (later the Royal) Photographic Society of London, with Queen Victoria and Prince Albert, always intrigued with modern novelties, as its first patrons. Its aim was to link professionals and amateurs, among whom were the Royal couple who had been instructed in the art by Roger Fenton (1819–69), first founder and secretary of the Society and best known for his Crimean War photographs. It was he who took the charming Royal portrait groups in 1854 which show a most elegant and well-tailored Albert and a Victoria wearing a flounced dress very typical of the feminine pretty styles that she favoured before her widowhood.

This was the great period of the amateur despite the very considerable cost and complexity of the process. In our context one of the best was Clementina Elphinstone, Lady Hawarden (1822–65). The pictures she took of her large family, which included several graceful good-looking daughters, bridge the gap between family and fashion photography and are particularly useful in their implied wry comment on the problems posed by the mode in the early 1860s. Possibly even Lady Hawarden's technique was stretched by the depth of focus needed to cope with large crinoline-supported skirts just as much as her daughters' skills were taxed by new and more complex hairstyles. Certainly the girls had off-days from elegance: skirts sag, crinolines bulge, silks are crumpled

and curls droop, but as a whole the groups have a most endearing humanity.

In general the amateur albums of albumen prints in so many of our public collections, most notably the Victoria and Albert Museum, show a much happier, more informal and relaxed person than the grim transfixed mannikin recorded by the average professional, who was notorious even amongst contemporaries for marooning his desperate client in the midst of ill-assorted mass-produced props. There are John Whistler's charming views of Hampshire country folk in the 1850s; there is the family from Scotland whose huntin', shootin' and fishin' activities are recorded, mostly between 1859 and 1869. Mr (later Alderman) Waterlow was in due course photographed in court suit and aldermanic robes, with both his plump serene wife and his mother, ever faithful to the pendent ringlets of the hairstyles of their respective youths. Mr H. Capper of Barham Court near Maidstone records servants, family and friends, and another dutiful young man collects and records first his fellow university students and then his pupils during the late 1860s and early 1870s, thus providing a great variety of illustrations of middle class boys' suiting. An album of the 1880s takes us into the world of faith and good works with teachers smart in the bustles of that time and children in their Sunday School best.

For always there are the children, peaceful and smiling. Early professionals dreaded juveniles. Even doubling the price could not compensate for all the wriggle and scream, and whenever possible they preferred to take the younger ones fast asleep. It was the skilled and loving amateur 'Lewis Carroll' (Charles Lutwidge Dodgson, 1832–98), in the photographs he took between 1856 and 1880, most notably in the 1860s, who conveyed the ease and happiness of the fortunate Victorian child. The clothes they wear – loose, short and comfortable – make them seem much closer to our own world than the stiff, flounced dwarfs of the fashion plates. And – an unexpected bonus for the dress historian – Dodgson found that flannel nightdresses (quite the rarest of historical survivals) posed an interesting textural problem for his camera and specifically instructed some Mamas to provide them for sittings! By the end of the period, technical improvements had made lively children less of a problem for the professional though a Leamington photographer was still prudently advising in his advertising calendar of 1881 that children should wear light coloured clothing and come to be photographed before noon, in the stronger morning light. By the end of the century the problems had been so far solved that according to the *Harmsworth Magazine* of 1899, Messrs F. & R. Speaight of Regent Street, specialists in child photography, had for two years been producing 'Baby's albums', regular and pre-booked records of Society's offspring.

The stark, sad images of the Dr Barnardo children convey the other side of Victorian childhood, the one known to the philanthropists. Possibly the practice originated in Scotland where William Smith photographer and Ragged Schoolmaster, photographed his first scholar, ragged, miserable and then redeemed, entitling it 'a day's transformation in 1858'. The waifs and strays were placed systematically on record from 1874, photographed on arrival at the Homes to assist in identification by parents – or police – and then again, rehabilitated, on departure. In the early photographs, sold at five shillings for a packet of six as tear-jerking purse-loosening publicity, they wear predictable rags which make them kin to the waifs in the Phiz illustrations to Charles Dickens, or the lad in *Lost*, posed and photographed so effectively by Oscar Gustave Rejlander (1813–75). After the Court case of 1868, questioning Dr Barnardo's publicity methods, the record settles to showing the children without sensationalism in the copious but ragged and ill-fitting clothing of the destitute. Within the Homes, the boys are shown in woollen suits and the girls in pinafores and dark warm dresses, or in the uniform peculiar to the institution.

For the mass of the population it was the introduction of the *carte de visite* which familiarised them with portrait photography. André Adolphe Disdèri (1819–90), the French photographer, had realised that multiple pictures on one plate could proportionately cut the cost of labour and materials, while the small size of the image would have the additional advantage of cutting out the need for expensive retouching. He patented his device in 1854 and it was to lower the price of prints by almost 90%. By the end of the decade it was in general use and in England a good photographer charged no more than a guinea a dozen for these small images and a cheap one only half as much.

At last the working classes, as well as the more affluent, could obtain a good and durable likeness. The upper classes are to be found in the Silvy and Bassano collections at the National Portrait Gallery while commercial archives, particularly those held by the Kodak Museum, Great Britain, provide an excellent cross-section of country and townsfolk between 1860 and 1900 as they wished to appear for their nearest and dearest. There are series from Cornwall, Warrington and Godmanchester, the first two dating from the early 1860s and the last from 1855 to 1900, though unfortunately dating must be by association for the negative guard books have been lost.

The most complete and potentially closely attributed set is still in private hands: the Boyer photographs lovingly cared for by a descendant of the photographer who took over his Sandwich studio and shop and was exhibited by the Science Museum, 1975–76, as 'William Boyer, Photographer at The Chain'. This has been called 'a microcosm of rural Victorian England', a complete cross-section of society from 1868 to 1896, recorded quite literally from the cradle to the grave, for it includes both babies and corpses. It is a mixed agricultural and maritime community and there are gentry, farmers, sailors, labourers, apprentices and household servants, 3,000 in all and many of them named. Boyer was quick to adapt to the dry plate process and from about 1884 there is an invaluable series of outdoor pictures in workshop, farm or hopfield. The documentary interest would be sufficient to make this a notable collection even without their considerable aesthetic quality. In the earlier set it is the men who show the greatest variety of clothing but in the later the style emphasis has shifted to the women.

The *carte de visite* was a great advance on the only other cheap form of photograph available, the ambrotype, a glass positive process introduced in 1854 and superficially similar in appearance to the daguerreotype, or the tintype or ferrotype, a positive on a metal plate. There are excellent examples of ambrotypes mainly in continental or American collections, but in England they seem to have fallen largely to the cheap 'sixpenny' photographers who so amusingly described their methods and techniques to Mayhew for his 1861 edition of *Life and Labour of the London Poor*. The images could be spurious as well as fragile and few of very good quality survive, though those that do are invaluable.

The *carte de visite*, a cheap and easy product, launched the craze of 'cartomania' which was to last until the end of the decade. From the Queen downwards everyone began to collect photographs of both friends and the famous. In 1869 the photographer S. B. Beale's list contains 1,019 celebrities and subjects ranging from Victoria herself to 'Beauties of the Ballet', all available for purchase at one shilling each. It was estimated that in England alone three to four hundred million were produced annually! Editions were enormous and W. Downey sold 300,000 copies of his 1867 picture of Alexandra, Princess of Wales with baby Louise on her back, while *cartes* from the John Jabez Mayall series *Royal Album* of 1860 and Camille Silvy's *Beauties of England* lend a touch of the fashionable, though anonymous and possibly misleading, elegance to many a dowdy provincial album.

Some celebrities updated their images by their willingness to sit: Alexandra was photographed at least once a year, providing soigné fashion comment on the change from 1860s crinolines to the bustle of the 1870s and '80s and the balloon sleeves of the 1890s. Others were more reluctant: Disraeli for example, agreed only at Queen Victoria's express insistence.

A characteristic of the process was that the same negative could contain several changes of pose. The proof sheets by Camille Silvy, the best-known portrait photographer of the time, now in the Victoria and Albert Museum collection, give several different views of the sitter and dress, as well as detail invisible in the average worn and faded copy to be found in most albums. Moreover, between 1859 and 1863 they have the additional advantage of being precisely datable, for his guard books are in the National Portrait Gallery, an excellent picture guide to high society from ladies in Court dress to babes in long clothes.

The mass-produced images of the *carte de visite* industry slot neatly into the Victorian publicity machine, which was moving into high gear in the latter part of the century, especially with the advent of respectable and popular journalism.

There was also the theatre which came of age in the 1860s when a talented series of actor-managers made it acceptable to the middle classes. This brought about a tremendous demand for pictures of actors and actresses as well as other celebrities. The young Jersey-born Lillie Langtry successfully 'crashed' London society in 1876, and, as shrewd as she was beautiful and hard-up, became the definitive

professional beauty when she sold exclusive rights to her photographs to Downey and Son. The Guy Little Collection in The Theatre Museum, supplemented by their other theatrical series, covers most stage personalities in and out of role, English and foreign, from the mid-nineteenth century, and provides ample material for a study of self-display and personal publicity in the second half of the century.

The techniques of the photographer were more than equal to the aesthetic and cosmetic demands made on them. Alfred Chalon, the miniaturist, might have told Queen Victoria 'Ah no, Madame, photographs cannot flattère' but he was hardly an unbiased commentator, and by the late 1850s lines and bulges could be dealt with quite easily either on negative or on print. However, a comparison between proof and finished copies suggests that retouching was not at all extensive. Photographers were sensitive to the client's desire for a 'Venus de Milo' brow, a 'flashing eye' and of course a 'lissom waist' but ridges above and below the corset and wrinkles in the dress seem to have bothered neither party. Perhaps they were too ubiquitous to be noticed. Even the self-consciously lovely Lillie was quite unaware of the bulges made by her bustle.

All the main London photographers produced pictures of the famous and beautiful, but Elliott and Fry, Alfred Ellis and Walery were the main theatrical specialists, the last selling prints from one-inch miniatures to 13-inch cabinets, costing from one shilling upwards, and the *Librairie Nilsson la référence des portraits contemporains*, which appeared annually between 1897 and 1905, provided a large and world-wide range of postage-stamp-sized images from the star-studded galaxy of the *fin de siècle* teenager's dream world, replete with romance as well as Royalty. The most daring are French but a chaste English eye, gaze averted from the voluptuously curving fleshings of La Belle Otèro, might still note that she was wearing a full-length fur coat, a great novelty in the 1890s.

There are so many portraits of the same sitters it is possible by comparison to see how experienced professionals from stage and studio working together could maximise the advantages of each sitting, switching pose and accessories to obtain the greatest variety of fashionable effect with the least expenditure of time and effort. Economy is commendable at any period but particularly so when a skirt might take 13 yards of material and a bodice only one! Examples of such contrivances abound in museums but are rarely illustrated in the magazine dressmaking columns of the period. Mrs Stirling wears a dress with high-cut day and low-cut evening bodice as does the tempestuous opera singer, Elena di Murska. Two outfits for the price of one and what a saving in storage and packing.

The importance of theatrical photographs to the history of dress at this period can hardly be overestimated. The audience expected realism in stage costume and appreciated an obvious, even laborious, attention to detail in contemporary as well as historical dramas. The costumes do not misrepresent, though in summarising for dramatic effect they may overstate. This too could affect the development of a fashion. E. A. Sothern as Lord Dundreary in *Our American Cousin* in 1858, with his droopy side whiskers, tiny bowler and chequer-board trousers both epitomised and promoted the clothes and behaviour of the exaggerated mid-Victorian 'heavy swell'.

Contemporaries were well aware of the interdependence of fashion and the theatre, and from the mid-1880s the journals carry regular features on clothes worn in the best-dressed plays, though in the early days English designers did not rate even a mention in the programme, let alone the press. In France, however, the designer was given almost as much billing as the playwright while actress and couturier would sometimes seem to have collaborated on a mutually congratulatory press release. The 'greats' of the theatre – Sarah Bernhardt, Madame Patti, Ellen Terry – toured indefatigably, stars of a truly international magnitude, and the fashion journalists and the clothing trade were not slow to capitalise: Madame Patti was given pre-season publicity clearance by the Chambre Syndicale de la Couture to take her Morin Blossier clothes to America in 1889. Lillie Langtry's toque and the Gaiety Girl Hat were no sooner worn than they were photographed, publicised and copied.

Despite this systematic and prolific exposure of the smart world, the fashion plate was not replaced by fashion photography until the very end of the period, even though such splendid large-plate pictures as those by James Arthur, now in the Kodak Museum, show that the camera could convey line and texture with luxurious and almost sensuous fidelity. It was used but only in a subordinate capacity and its acceptance was slow and partial. Engravers had used photography for illustration reference since the early days of its introduction and in the later 1860s portraits of well-known personalities of the day were used as models for the engraved heads in clothing advertisements, wittingly or unwittingly endorsing the product. Indeed it is surprising that the celebrities, whose likenesses lithographed from photographs appear thrust through the collars of Samuel Bros' cheap slop-tailored suits in their 1868 catalogue *Illustrative Portraiture Groups, Princes, Poets and Painters*, never sued for defamation of character.

The earliest use of photography as a commercial garment record is in the Public Record Office in the Register of Useful and Ornamental Designs, where the firm of W. C. Jay of Regent Street used it to record the design of a mantle in 1857. Their example was followed in 1872 by the army which by sending out three way views of the new-type military tunic saved on the making of 200 pattern garments. By the late 1880s the French couture house of Worth was photographing dresses on stands as a house record of designs. These are now in the Design Archive of the National Art Library, Victoria and Albert Museum, and it seems reasonable to suppose that they were also copied by the fashion artists, though no definitive evidence remains to support this. What is certain is that by the later 1870s photographs of theatrical personalities were being engraved direct as fashion plates. Madame Thea's photograph in a fur-trimmed skating dress of surely inhibiting tightness appears engraved as an anonymous fashion plate in the *Englishwoman's Domestic Magazine* of 1876. The Sarony picture of Madame Patti in one of her pre-release concert dresses of 1888, engraved in the *Woman's World* of the same year, demonstrates the not-so-minor modifications that were necessary to turn even a handsome reality into a fashion-plate ideal. The dashing William Terris proved less of a problem when his photograph was engraved for reproduction as an illustration of the 'Tattersall Vest' by *West End Fashions* in 1887.

The reasons were in part aesthetic. Even after the turn of the century fashion artists still noted with some satisfaction that photography made the ladies look fat. Engravings were also economical, for retouching was expensive. But the major reason was technical. Cheap photographic reproduction suitable for the news or periodical press did not really come into use until the end of the century even though photogravure had been introduced in 1880. An important and little-known pioneer in the use of direct photography for fashion promotion was the London shop of Peter Robinson who 'tipped in' photographs in their mourning catalogue as early as 1865. They are prints of very high quality, amazingly clear and successful in imparting charm to all-black gowns hardly designed to enhance. In 1876 they put together a series of *cartes de visite* with pictures of models in the gowns with details of price and material imprinted on the back. They were well ahead of any foreign competitors: the first French example in photogravure and by 'Nadar' – and a rather lumpy model at that – did not appear in *L'Art et la Mode* until 1881. Attractive as the Peter Robinson pictures are, the example does not seem to have been followed. Moreover, the fashion plate artists with 300 years of experience behind them were skilled, available and cheap.

Peter Robinson's success is all the more surprising in that the camera always had been rather particular, not to say exclusive, about the clothes it photographed. 'Cuthbert Bede', waggishly Victorian, comments in 1855 that 'King Camera prescribes his court costume'. There were two basic problems: the difficulties of calculating an exposure when extreme contrasts of black and white were involved – and these were common in Victorian dress – and the way that colour registered on the negative plate. Early photographs are the victims of colour bias and Mr Brian Coe of the Kodak Museum suggests that this can be simulated by viewing through a deep blue filter. Green, yellow, orange and red all appear dark, and pale blue as white. In the 1860s the contrasts seem more dramatic in photographs than they do in surviving garments. Not until the introduction of the orthochromatic and the isochromatic plate in the 1880s was the emulsion sensitive to green, while red appeared black until the panchromatic plate came into use in the late 1890s.

The problems were serious enough for Mayall and Beard, the early daguerreotypists, to attempt to persuade their sitters to wear clothing provided by the studio, which was not at all popular with their clientele! Possible confusion may arise from the Victorian convention that even married and mature sisters might dress alike but on the whole unrelated ladies in the same dress would be considered as evidence of a strong-minded photographer or an unusually early example of Victorian mass-produced ready-to-wear. The photographer's usual remedy was to pester the sitters with good advice.

In 1846, Dr Andrew Wynter, writing in the *People's Journal*, advised those sitting for a daguerreotype to:

avoid pure white as much as possible. Some ladies dress themselves out in snowy berthas and spotless wrist bands, but many a good picture is spoiled by the spottiness occasioned by the powerful action of this colour upon the plate. Violets have the same effect on it. A lady takes her sitting in a purple dress and is astonished to find herself in white muslin in her portrait ... The very best kind of dress to wear ... is satin or shot-silk, or any material, in fact, upon which there is a play of light or shade. Plaids always look well and an old tartan shawl thrown across the shoulders ... would form an admirable drapery but this is an artistic liberty which ladies are very loath to submit to ... We wish ladies would be a little less prim on such occasions. It is quite melancholy to see the care they take to brush their hair and apply that abomination fixiture [sic] to make it look nice. And let them ... abjure the system of making up a face for the occasion. The effect is painfully transparent.

Successful Mr Mayall with his large and popular studio was too busy to be other than explicit and Bede informs us that in the 1850s 'Suggestions for dress' were handed to all his clients. They bear out Dr Wynter's instructions:

Ladies are informed that dark silks and satins are best for dress; shot-silk, checked, striped or figured material provided that they be not too light, and colours to be avoided are white, light blue and pink. The only dark colour to be avoided is black velvet. *For gentlemen*: black, figured check or plaid or other fancy vests are preferable to white. *For children*: plaid, striped red or figured dresses.

And since the chief tabooed colour was white, brides and clergymen in surplices, so Bede informs us, would appear as 'so many ghosts'. This certainly applies to the rare mid-century photograph of a white-clad bride, but Mr Mayall must have gone to considerable trouble to retouch the charming portrait of Alexandra in her wedding dress in 1863. Presumably Mayall also knew how to cope with the small light dress cap, the conventional indoor accessory of the married or mature, unlike some of the less competent professional photographers. *Household Words* in 1855 is heavily humorous on the incongruity of portraits of old ladies minus their headgear, fastening unerringly on the bizarre results of an imperfect taste or technique.

Nevertheless the quantity of tartan waistcoats, patterned silk and moiré dresses in fashion plates and museum collections confirms that their presence in photographic portraits is a fair reflection of reality. The technical problem also explains the small numbers of evening dresses shown. They were not avoided on moral grounds as too frivolous for posterity but because the fashionable light sugary colours did not lend themselves to reproduction.

By the end of the century techniques had so far improved that, as reported by the *Harmsworth Magazine* of 1899, Alice Hughes, the Society portrait photographer, preferred the ladies and children in whom she specialised to wear white or at least light colours.

For a more varied record of the dress of the mid-nineteenth century, however, we must turn from the portrait to the genre scene. The best known are the stereo photographs at their most popular and prolific between 1851 and 1867. Two slightly divergent images were focused through a special viewer, and provided a vivid 'in-depth' view of the world without need to step outside the parlour. The temptation to compare the craze with the television today is irresistible. One critic writing in 1858 calls them 'absurd made up subjects'; others were more appreciative: 'we have ... looked through a three inch lens at every single pomp and vanity of this wicked world'. The most useful from the fashion point of view are probably the 'absurd made up subjects': genre scenes in studio sets with crowded and obviously posed groups of widely flounced ladies wedged in between over-stuffed furniture. They have anecdotal titles and a set may form a gently comic sequence. A high proportion were produced by the London Stereoscopic Company of Regent Street. Although they provide a comprehensive picture of completely accessorised clothing within a social context, the groups as a whole are not necessarily realistic. Some, like the crinoline set, are linked with contemporary caricatures while others reflect, though with some distortion, popular paintings.

The link between Victorian painting and photography was in any case a close one. Artist and public admired a reality painstakingly recreated, preferably with moral overtone, and as a work of art was respected in proportion to its attention to detail, its creation had to be almost demonstrably toilsome. Photographers like Henry Peach Robinson (1830–1901) meticulously linked photographic studies into composite 'pictures', as appealing to contemporaries for their concept and ingenuity as for their sincerity. The compilations are artificial but the elements realistic, and of his 'Bringing Home the May', the *Photographic Journal* of 1862 applauded the 'homely garb of actual life'.

While photographers used painterly concepts to form their compositions, so in their turn painters made use of photographs. As early as 1845, Ruskin, the most influential art critic of his period, described photography, in this context, as 'a most blessed invention', and Hill's adoption of the calotype has already been described. William Frith, that most popular painter and a typical man of his time, notes consistently in his autobiography the effort involved and the profit from his large-scale and popular works: 'The Railway Station' required two years' work, though it earned him £4,500. He also details his trials and tribulations with his models, sometimes tipsy, usually late, occasionally dishonest and frequently grasping. Small wonder that he was seduced by the prepackaged reality of the photograph. Although his efforts to use it for 'Ramsgate Sands', 1852, were unsuccessful, he had better luck with 'Derby Day', 1854–56, when the *Journal of the Photographic Society*, 16 January 1863, reported that he 'employed his kind friend Mr Howlett to photograph for him from the roof of a cab, as many queer groups of figures as he could'. He used it for 'The Railway Station', 1860–62, and much more systematically for the absentee or fidgety subjects needed for 'The Wedding of the Prince of Wales', 1863–64. Few of the photographs survive, and he did not stress their use, which could possibly be construed as attempts to dodge the moral obligations of hard work, but there are sufficient to confirm the clothes conventions and reciprocal realism of the photographs and his paintings, mirrors of the mid-Victorian world.

Mere 'photographic realism' however was *not* regarded as art and on this score the pre-Raphaelites were criticised by their contemporaries, but the set of portraits of Mrs William Morris, posed by Dante Gabriel Rossetti for Maynard, the photographer, on a sunny July afternoon of 1865, do credit to the artist, independent of his medium. There is a direct link between at least two of the poses and paintings, 'La Pia de Tolomei', 1865, and 'Reverie', 1868, but in our context their main interest is the clothes worn by Jane Morris. They are early examples of dress modified by aesthetic concepts but it is the absence of the crinoline, the minimal trimming, rather than any eccentricity of cut, which provide their distinction. Jane Morris's magnificent bush of hair, her swan-like throat, are quite sufficient on their own to impart an other-worldly quality even to the quite conventional if rather old-fashioned flounced dress with pagoda sleeves which she wears for two of the photographs.

It is interesting to compare her clothes with the better-known aesthetic reform dress of the next generation as depicted in Frith's 'Private View at the Royal Academy', 1882. The most charming of the aesthetic group is Ellen Terry, who appears in a loose-fitting balloon-sleeved 'sack' almost identical to that in which she was photographed during the same period, and to judge from later prints, this unwaisted style was one from which she never departed. Possibly it was the influence of her 'husbands' – Frederick Watts and E. W. Godwin, both pioneers of the dress reform movement – or perhaps she just hated the constriction of corsets. In the Academy group she stands by Oscar Wilde, that modish apostle of aestheticism, dressed here in the smart frock coat of the fashionable play-wright, journalist and man-about-town, not in the 'aesthetic' jacket and knee-breeches which had so shocked the ribald Philistines of America during his lecture tour in 1882. He was photographed in both outfits. Another of Ellen Terry's reformer friends, the young Bernard Shaw, was also placed on record wearing his jersey Jaeger suit in which, it was said, he looked like a bifurcated radish.

Thus far Disraeli's second nation, the people, have appeared in front of the camera as principals only if they could spare the sixpenny minimum charge of a professional photo-grapher, and until 1860 few of their likenesses survive. The only chance of achieving immort-ality was as 'extras' if they had an amateur as an employer, constantly on the watch for obedient subjects. Now they appear as acolytes in the transcendental industrial enterprises of which this period was so proud. Clothed in the dignity of labour and almost inevitably the chimney-pot hat, they were photographed by Philip H. Delamotte (1820–89) reconstructing the Crystal Palace at Sydenham, 1851–54, and by

Robert Howlett and J. Cundall launching the *Great Eastern* in 1857. The building of the 1862 Exhibition was also recorded. Apart from these there seems to have been a feeling that they tended to spoil the picture. Vernon Heath, a good professional of his time, was amazed to be importuned and offered a guinea by an old apple woman who wished to be included in his record of the installation of the Landseer lions in Trafalgar Square in 1864: 'what her motive was I could not divine – at all events, when I refused she looked very disappointed'. A feeling we share, for no apple woman was to find herself immortalised in photograph for another decade.

Increasingly from the 1850s poorer people were marshalled in front of the camera in the interests of that new science, Social Research. Dr Barnardo's work in this field has already been mentioned. Their earliest appearance was as daguerreotype sources for engravings in the illustrated papers, and quite systematically in the first 1851 edition of Henry Mayhew's *Life and Labour of the London Poor*. Here, the vast majority of the illustrations were captioned quite specifically as having been taken from daguerreotypes by Beard. In the 1861 edition the series expanded to include engravings made from 'photographs', presumably collodion negatives. A letter in which Mayhew asks permission to send a photographer to record a prison scene still exists. Incidentally he pro-mised to alter the faces. Undoubtedly props and background were added: the sewer man in his drain would have been inaccessible before the introduction of efficient flash, not available until the very end of the century. It is interesting to compare the picturesque sewer man with the late-nineteenth century Cornish tin miners in their unexceptional overalls, taken by J. C. Burrow, a pioneer of flashlight photography, for his *'mongst Mines and Miners*, 1893.

Not until 1877 is there another attempt to record the town-dweller: John Thomson (1837–1921) and Adolphe Smith's *Street Life in London* produced with 'permanent photo-graphic illustrations take from life expressly for this publication'. They are Woodbury-types and have a great clarity of detail. Contempor-aries comment on the scarifying social realism but it is the pictorial images by Thomson, explorer and photographer, not Smith's rather gossipy text, which give it impact and makes its value enduring.

The rural unfortunate were recorded by Dr H. W. Diamond (1809–86), Resident Superintendent of Female Patients at the Surrey County Asylum (1848–58) and Secretary-Editor of the Royal Photographic Society. His aim was to catch 'the passing storm or sunshine of the soul', and hopefully to obtain insight into the philosophy of the human mind. His large, clear photographs, published in 1856 as *Physiognomy of Insanity*, show the women wearing not the formless rags of the more scarifying 'realist' painters, for some wear straw hats and print dresses, everyday country garb, which almost never survives in costume collections.

Working women form the nucleus of the groups brought together by Arthur J. Munby (1828–1910), whose obsessional life-long concern with the woman manual worker led him to make a systematic and annotated collection of their likenesses, now housed in Trinity College Library, Cambridge. To him, the most important series were of general servants, most frequently Hannah, whom he courted from 1862 and married ten years later. He found the lilac printed dress, frilled cap and apron of the middle class domestic servant profoundly affecting. He was also intrigued by the Wigan pit girls, lustily handsome in their working breeches and striped skirts, as well as fisherwomen, mostly from the north east coast, London milk-carriers and an assorted group of more miscellaneous toilers. Of particular interest are the prints of the girls in their best clothes, which appear indistinguishable in style and material from those of the middle and upper classes. The Pilkington Album of the workers from the St Helens glass works confirms such smartness to be unexceptional. Even the experienced Munby had to depend on deportment and observation of large and toil-worn hands to distinguish his candidates. He never could sort our ladies' maids from their mistresses. He could and did sketch, but he was not a photographer; for at this period it was an expensive hobby, and all the paraphernalia necessary might have seriously compromised his informal friendly relationship with the girls, who affectionately – and perhaps warily – regarded him as 'the inspector'. It was cheaper and easier when he saw one whose appearance interested him to tip her a shilling for her trouble and pay for the sitting.

The same detail and humanity is to be found in the better-known work of Frank M. Sutcliffe (1853–1941), 'the pictorial Boswell of Whitby', whose photographs are perhaps the most frequently reproduced of the nineteenth cen-

tury. He was the local professional and progressed from portraits to local scenes and people. He is said to have waited for the groups that he wanted to occur naturally, taking advantage of the brief exposure possible with the gelatine dry plate. It can be assumed that the people shown, though selected, are typical for their area or occupation. However, the trial 'snapshot' prints taken for Kodak suggest that the fisherfolk tidied themselves up considerably for the better known and more publicised pictures. The women show little sign of any local peculiarity of dress except for their sunbonnets, or much consciousness of fashion, but such as it is, it is confined to the sleeveheads of their blouses which become fuller throughout the 1890s. The men dress like those in Thomson, but, as is to be expected, their clothes are tidier and better made. Characteristic of the district are the fishermen in sou'westers, thigh-length sea boots and the distinctively patterned knitted jumpers which were a speciality of the area until the influx of naval surplus after the Second World War, and are now a local craft revived. By contrast, Hill and Adamson's fishermen in tarred top hats and canvas slops look back to the age of Nelson.

Sutcliffe's photographs were widely admired and exhibited in his own day, and had many followers and imitators, amateurs and professionals, sometimes derisively dubbed the 'Cottage Door School'.

A study might yield information on local variations of style, though the photographers were not above putting their friends in picturesque items from the fancy-dress box.

Two hundred miles to the south, Peter Henry Emerson (1856–1936) was recording the Norfolk Broads in the interests of what he termed 'naturalistic photography', inspired by his admiration for French painting and his dislike for the re-created reality, the pose and props of Rejlander and Henry Peach Robinson, excluding all means but the photographic. His figure studies of what, with some condescension, he referred to as 'the typical Norfolk peasant' appear looming against the subtle tones of the background, in *Life and Landscape on the Norfolk Broads*, 1887. Their clothes are characteristic of Norfolk dress: the men wearing boat smocks, jean jackets and long boots, the women the mid-calf length skirts of the marsh-dweller and belted hip-length blouses, but numerically his actual cast is so limited that it is impossible to say whether the high-crowned bonnet and rather rakish man's felt hat are local peculiarities or have wider currency. He was not the most unobtrusive of men or photographers, and there must have been more than enough advance warning for his subjects to have got cleaned up even if they did not actually change their clothes for their appearance before his large plate camera conveyed so precariously and painfully through the marsh. Despite his protestation, his subject photographs are closer to the sanitised and bowdlerised world of Victorian subject painting than they are to the gritty reality of the French landscape school.

Their limitation as a record is emphasised by comparison with the work of Sir George Clausen (1852–1944), Professor of Painting at South Kensington, not merely a disciple of Millet but an actual pupil through Bastien Lepage and conscious both of the importance of realistic detail and its subordination to the effect of the picture as a whole. In pursuit of visual truth, he traversed the countryside not only with a sketch-book and pencil, but also one of the new hand cameras capable of 'snapping' at a speed of 1/50th of a second, and taking his subjects completely unposed and unaware. Here at last is the agricultural labourer as he appeared to his neighbours. What we notice are the shabby miscellaneous garments, and the scrawny toil-worn bodies. Here is a true portrait of rural England in the period of decline, so stark that Clausen found it necessary to prettify it in his paintings.

Cameras such as the one he used were produced in response to the public craving for something convenient and unobtrusive. The gelatine dry plate invented in 1871 by Richard Leach Maddox (1816–1902) and John Burgess, which became commercially available in the 1880s, was as much as 20 times as fast as the wet collodion process and for the first time instant photography at speeds of less than a second became possible. Bromide papers simplified and accelerated developing and at last photographers were free from all that cumbersome load of paraphernalia.

Fenton's Crimean wine merchant's van, studio and darkroom combined, postcard pioneer Francis Frith's packing cases of gear so perspiringly toted up the Nile, Vernon Heath peeking though the ivy to catch Miss Burdett Coutts' garden party guests unselfconscious and unaware, receded unregretted into the past. Photography became much easier though it was still not sufficiently simple or inexpensive to

become a popular pastime and, as George Eastman, the American photographic business pioneer, realised, until it became really popular it could not become really profitable.

The age of the 'snapshot' arrived with the No. 1 Kodak camera which Eastman introduced in 1888. By using the new celluloid-based roll film, fixed-focus lens, single speed and stop and reducing the former ten complicated procedures to a simple three, the last technical barriers were removed. Anyone could take photographs almost anywhere, and the forces of big business were there to see that you did. 'You press the button, we do the rest' promised the Kodak company, and thousands of amateurs proceeded to do just that.

The expansive mid-Victorian had been happy to record the wonders of the universe but the somewhat sadder and wiser inhabitants of a *fin de siècle* world were encouraged to make 'a pictorial record of life as it is lived'. Unfortunately, many were too snap-happy to make a good photograph and too euphoric to document the result, but that was the beginning of the family snapshot album as we know it today.

One amateur beyond reproach was Benjamin Stone (1838–1914), Birmingham business man, Conservative politician, traveller and amateur photographer whose work was commemorated by an exhibition at the National Portrait Gallery in 1974. Stone had systematically collected pictures of the places to which he had travelled from 1863 to 1880, but on his first world trip he began to take his own photographs, taking with him, in addition to more conventional equipment, a No. 1 Kodak camera. Home again, he took many family groups representative of the aristocracy and plutocracy of the Midlands, not clad in high fashion perhaps but wearing good middle of the road clothes of the period. He recorded house parties, christenings and weddings, where the more sensitive late-nineteenth century emulsion restored the white bride to the land of the living. The photographs, meticulously named and dated, are visual comment on late Victorian *mores*: the generation gap, for instance, is less apparent than it is today. The affluent middle-aged of the last quarter of the nineteenth century are relatively smarter than their great-grandchildren would be in a similar situation. A small cap marks mature status, and if the flesh is too weak or gross to bear the rigours of stout corseting, then an up-to-date sleeve proclaims some awareness of fashion.

From 1897 when he became an MP until his

death, it was Stone's self-imposed task to record every inhabitant of the Palace of Westminster and most important visitors. It is a superb pictorial survey of the man of the late nineteenth century. There are ladies, mainly with their husbands, having tea on the terrace, but on the whole they are typical and add little we do not already know. He photographed his subjects exactly as he found them. The *Amateur Photographer and Photographic News* of 1 May 1911 found his attitude disconcerting: 'I should hesitate before submitting to the *Tailor and Cutter* Sir Benjamin Stone's photographs of individual legislators! He insists on taking his subjects standing, and upon showing the whole man, baggy trouser knees, clumsy boots and all'. As it happened the *Tailor and Cutter* found such records just as fascinating as we do – if for rather different reasons – and until the First World War they printed regular and quite often critical accounts of the clothes of the country's elected representatives.

Unconsciously or consciously – and this was an age by no means unaware of the power of the media – the politicians project their images and their political affiliations in stance and dress: Keir Hardie and John Burns, first of the Socialists, wear thick, ill-fitting – and very well publicised – lounge suits similar to the clothes worn by the subjects of Thomson and Paul Martin. Austen Chamberlain, suave and elegant, fitting representative of Birmingham, the Venice of the Midlands, and the aristocracy of trade, wears a beautifully-fitted frock coat.

Benjamin Stone's passion for recording encompassed the national scene when, after intitiating the Warwickshire photographic survey in 1890, he embarked on the National Photographic Record Association with the aim of recording all objects of interest in the British Isles and placing the prints, annotated and documented, unaltered by retouching, in the British Museum. This project attracted no government support, and gradually the effort separated into small groups to the great benefit of local archives. Sir Benjamin saw history as a series of pictures in daily danger of destruction and consciously tried to record contemporary events, especially unusual and local customs – Morris dances, May Days and such, which he feared would soon disappear – though, unless they were participants, people as such are hardly featured. Despite the partial failure of his original scheme, more than any other photographer he succeeded in providing an accessible visual record of his own time and his prints may be seen upon request at either the British Museum Department of Prints and Drawings, the National Portrait Gallery or the Birmingham Central Library. Oddly enough, his popularisation *Sir Benjamin Stone's Pictures*, 1900–05, is relatively difficult to find.

Paul Martin (1864–1944), dubbed the 'Victorian candid camera man', used Clausen's method to do for the man in the street what Stone had attempted for the nation. He was an engraver and print-maker, and in 1891 began to specialise in photographs of everyday life, purchasing one of the new small Facile Hand Cameras, camouflaging its still fairly considerable bulk and four-pound weight by disguising it as a parcel. His earliest work, a series of 'One-man Businesses' in the City of London which he took during his lunch-times in 1890, should be compared with the engravings in Mayhew, but this workaday world is drab and there is a greater sartorial contrast between artisan and bourgeois than there seems to have been a generation before. Martin's street-traders are Thomson's East-Enders a decade later. Though style has changed dramatically it has affected them hardly at all. There is only a faint echo of the vertical emphasis of the fashion line of the late 1880s. The men's clumsy lounge suits are marginally higher-waisted and tighter cut; women's skirts scantier and their bonnets worn higher on the head. It is Martin's seaside and bank-holiday scenes, not his workaday ones, which illustrate the slight but real improvement in working-class living standards which had taken place by the end of the nineteenth century. The higher wages, shorter hours, and a new concept, the annual paid holiday, were all to affect the course of fashion in the years to come. There are beach scenes: the girls in their smart new clothes with 'leg of mutton'-sleeved blouses and ankle-length skirts, spooning with their boy friends on the sands, hats and bonnets well anchored against the stiff sea breezes. The lads wear striped blazers, matching ties, light ankle-length trousers and jaunty straw boaters, very much the clothes which 20 years before could only have been sported by the middle classes. Everywhere there are children, not the scrawny, pale throw-backs to Dr Barnardo-type waifs of his urban scenes, but carefree, laughing, with the breeze blowing petticoat and knicker frill while they paddle in the shallows.

There is an intimacy and vivacity in Martin's

work, particularly apparent in his Hampstead Heath bank holiday scenes taken in 1895. The costers and their girl friends, better known perhaps in the black and white drawing of his contemporary, Phil May, are still the distinctively dressed sub-group so carefully described by Mayhew. The girls wear large feather-trimmed hats like those of the ritually-dressed Pearly Queens of today and ankle-length, slightly bustled, back-fastening dresses, somewhat archaic in cut. Their escorts are distinguished by velvet bum-freezer coats, peaked caps and mufflers, and just to give the final satisfaction to the student of fashion, voyeur Martin walks around the laughing line of dancers and records them from the rear.

The immediacy, the unusual angle of vision, the sense of movement and detail of these photographs, lead inevitably to the moving picture – the cinema – which was already foreshadowed in the work of Eadweard Muybridge (1830–1904), the English-born photographer who worked in America. He undertook an *Electrophotographic investigation of consecutive phases of animal movement* between 1872 and 1885, recording it in a series of split-second exposures linked by a set of electronic trip wires and photographing from different angles. He had demonstrated his 'motion pictures' throughout Europe in 1887, as the 'Zoopraxiscope'. The experiment, undertaken with the co-operation of the University of Pennsylvania, is best known for its animal studies like the galloping horse, but among the 900 sets of photographs are many groups of figures. Those who wear clothes are distinguished by the letter (d) in the systematic list which accompanies the sets of plates. The experiment, though undoubtedly serious and very systematic, seems to have been undertaken in a reasonably light-hearted way and the figures, whether student or professional models, good-humouredly engage in numerous activities, sweeping floors, playing tennis, sitting down, climbing stairs, throwing balls, each gesture and movement of the body viewed from at least three angles. The clothes of the 1880s are often considered to be the most stiff and cumbersome of the entire nineteenth century, but despite the severe chimney-pot hats, the rigid bustles, the tight corseting, the girls are quite amazingly lissom and lithe, considering the quantities of garments which we not only know them to have been wearing, but which, in some of the photographs, we can see being put on and taken off. Here is a real keyhole view of dress.

The whole of human life is here; by the end of the nineteenth century the camera could record anyone doing anything at any place and at any time. From the photographic point of view there is no reason why the record of people and their clothes should not be both universal and complete, provided good fortune attends the search.

Ladies' Dress

The 1840s

1 William Fox Talbot photographed his mother in 1841 wearing a dress very similar to this. The technique of photography was new, but the dress and the substantial parasol are slightly old fashioned, with the full sleeves and belted, medium-high waist making it much closer to the fashions of the 1830s. With it she wears a flower-trimmed, deep-crowned bonnet

2 Lady Feilding, relaxing in a caped floral pattern dressing gown and elaborate indoor cap. The cap, medium-deep and flat-crowned, is reasonably fashionable for the early 1840s, the date of this photograph, but the forehead curls, suspiciously dark and luxuriant for a lady of her years, tight inner cap and the small floral pattern, high waist and full sleeves are more Regency than early Victorian. It is the sort of time lag to be expected in the clothes of an elderly lady

3 A study of lace from Fox Talbot's *The Pencil of Nature*, the example he used to demonstrate the sharpness of a negative image. The precision is sufficient to allow identification of the lace as a machine copy of English bobbin, with hand-run border to the design. Such trimmings were purchased ready made and by the yard, and used to edge caps, collars and cuffs

Above opposite
4 All the females of the Fox Talbot household seem to have contributed to this prototype record photograph of feminine millinery of the early 1840s. This is probably a parallel series to the China Closet illustration in *The Pencil of Nature*. Starting at the top, from left to right there is a shaped collar, an evening wreath, a flower-trimmed cap, a flower and another wreath. On the next shelf down are three caps and an evening bandeau with a rosette at each side, while below there are three caps and another wreath on the far right. On the bottom shelf are the bonnets, the first of a drawn or gathered silk, the next trimmed with gathered net, then a smaller straw bonnet trimmed with flowers, a larger and more old fashioned one, and finally another in more up-to-date style and trimmed with gathered silk and ribbon. The indoor caps of the period were often, though not always, made by the wearer or her maid, and are fragile confections of net wired to a shape and trimmed with lace, often silk 'blonde', ribbon ruches and/or flowers. The drawn bonnets were sometimes made on the same principle, but straw, velvet or plush shapes could be bought plain and trimmed up at home. Mrs Gaskell's *Cranford* contains many insights into the importance of pretty millinery in a limited wardrobe. Caps became less common among younger women in the 1840s but when worn for visiting were carried to and fro in a box or basket

5 A fashionable bonnet of the mid-1840s with contrast looped ribbon and feather trimming can be seen very clearly in this portrait study of Lady Constance Talbot. It is similar in essentials to the one shown in figure 1, deep and straight-crowned, and worn so that the brim entirely obliterates the profile

an informal day cap, wired to shape and with trimming at ear level, and covering a coiffure similar to that shown so clearly in the other view – centre parted with the side hair drawn over the front of the ear before being looped up to a small bun at the back of the head

Opposite

8 and **9** The Fox Talbot family in the early and the mid-1840s. In figure 8, in tea time pose, they still wear the clothes which, fashionable in the late 1830s, have now become rather out-of-date, similar to those we have already seen on the ladies in figures 1 and 2. The bodices are high-waisted – the stiff line of the corset clearly seen in the lady seated in profile – the sleeves full from elbow to wrist, and the skirts not over-voluminous. Each lady wears a differently shaped collar, and indeed the second quarter of the nineteenth century exhibits lingerie of great delicacy and in great variety. All wear indoor caps, semi-transparent and trimmed at ear level. Standing to the left is William Henneman, Fox Talbot's personal servant, assistant and the subject of many photographs. He wears a light coloured morning coat with metal buttons and an 'M' notch rolling lapel. Fox Talbot himself, seated, is, as always, very smart, with notably well fitted trousers strapped beneath the foot. He wears his top

6 and **7** Lady formal by Claudet and lady informal, by Fox Talbot, probably taken in the mid-1840s. Both are fashionable and wear dresses with fairly tight sleeves, slightly trimmed at the elbows, with pointed waists and gently full skirts. The more formal lady reading (6), wears a low-cut silk dress, the neck trimmed with a triple-row lace flounce. The striped day dress (7), is a higher cut and has a white needlework collar. The sitter also wears

hat, at this period tall and straight sided. On the whole it was not normal to wear a hat in a domestic situation like this, and his motivation is not clear, unless it is to demonstrate his contention that 'when carefully posed, people can be trained to maintain sufficient stillness for the necessary duration of the exposure'. By him stands a messenger-cum-servant, wearing a great coat and with hat in hand.

By the mid-1840s the ladies of the Fox Talbot family seem to have caught up with fashion and have acquired dresses with longer waists and tighter sleeves. All wear pretty collars and aprons, the latter a popular informal accessory which saved the dress from soiling. Only the oldest lady wears a cap, and the different poses of the others allow several different views of the coiffure characteristic of the 1840s. The girls in profile dress their front hair differently; the one who is kneeling has it dressed in ringlets, the other has it plaited and looped up to her bun

10 This daguerreotype of an unknown lady of the mid-1840s sharpens up the image already seen in the calotypes. The dress is conventional in cut and fabric, and with it the lady wears a contrast bonnet with floral trimming inside the brim at ear level and a light paisley patterned shawl. Her jewellery is restrained and she wears a cameo brooch at the neck and an eyeglass on what looks like a mixed metal and hair chain

11 Miss Crampton assumes a fashion plate-like pose for her Edinburgh photograph by Hill and Adamson in 1843–47. Her dress of horizontally striped silk is fashionably cut and the trimming which extends from the bodice drape into the skirt elongates the line. Miss Crampton wears a cap and carries one of the fashionable small parasols. Her bonnet is posed so that the ribbons and floral trimmings are visible. She wears a long narrow shawl, possibly of silk, and a heavier tartan wrap is arranged as a decorative drape on the right of the picture

12 Mrs Rigby and her daughter were photographed by Hill and Adamson during one of their visits to Edinburgh in the mid-1840s. Mrs Rigby wears a handsome damask dress, the floral pattern of which is perhaps easier to make out in other photographs from this session. With it she wears a double collar, whose decoration of open work embroidery and 'gothic' dentillated border is more characteristic of the previous decade. Her daughter is very fashionable and her shorter rounded waist and full double-skirted dress anticipate the more bouffant line of the 1850s. The older lady wears a cap reminiscent of those seen in the Fox Talbot series, her daughter one of the new smaller bonnets and a shawl with paisley pattern borders

13 and 14 Mr Monro and Mrs Gallie photographed by Hill and Adamson in the mid-1840s. Mr Monro is dressed with formal elegance in a full-skirted frock coat, high dark cravat and a tartan velvet double-breasted waistcoat with the pattern arranged so that it mimics the triangular ladies' bodice line. His check tweed trousers, straight and rather narrow, are anchored beneath the foot with a strap. His square-toed boots have galoche tops in contrasting texture. Mrs Gallie is equally formal in a low-necked tartan silk dress with Bertha collar and a narrow shawl. Her coiffure, with is long face-framing curls, was popular both with the young and for formal occasions. The back view shows even more clearly how the style is arranged. Divested of her shawl she

has a fashion plate elegance and her swan like neck is emphasised by the low shoulder line. A detail usually glossed over by fashion plates is the ridge left by the low cut corset, which is sufficiently tight to displace a roll of flesh on even a slender figure. The medium-full skirt must owe its extra back fullness to the addition of a bustle. She carries a fan with a feather border

15 An unknown lady in a daguerreotype of the late 1840s provides a very clear view of the essentials of 1840s style, with its very tight low-set sleeves and full skirt gathered to a low waist line. The bodice is precisely seamed and adjusted to a torso constricted by the narrow-waisted corset which holds the body in a stiff, unnaturally tilted position. The hairstyle so characteristic of the decade, with its down sweep in front of the ear, is particularly well illustrated

16 and **17** Kit Talbot, William Fox Talbot's brother, with his wife and daughter, were photographed by William probably in 1848. Mrs Talbot wears a dress with the small geometric pattern popular in the period, and a basqued jacket whose contrast soft frilly trimming looks forward to the softer styles of the 1850s. Its front is protected by a satin dress apron. Her daughter wears the sort of low, tight dress of which the reformers disapproved, short socks and side-button light-topped boots. Kit Talbot's clothes are similar to those worn by Mr Monro (13) but his waistcoat is straight-cut and single-breasted. It is difficult to explain the saggy droop of his light straight-cut trousers, except to suggest that for some reason best known to himself he has taken off his braces – the waist does seem to bulge in a rather haphazard way

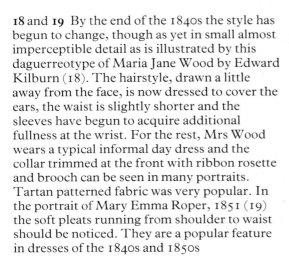

18 and 19 By the end of the 1840s the style has
begun to change, though as yet in small almost
imperceptible detail as is illustrated by this
daguerreotype of Maria Jane Wood by Edward
Kilburn (18). The hairstyle, drawn a little
away from the face, is now dressed to cover the
ears, the waist is slightly shorter and the
sleeves have begun to acquire additional
fullness at the wrist. For the rest, Mrs Wood
wears a typical informal day dress and the
collar trimmed at the front with ribbon rosette
and brooch can be seen in many portraits.
Tartan patterned fabric was very popular. In
the portrait of Mary Emma Roper, 1851 (19)
the soft pleats running from shoulder to waist
should be noticed. They are a popular feature
in dresses of the 1840s and 1850s

1850–1864

20 A daguerreotype of an unknown lady, *circa* 1850, shows her wearing a dress with a small floral pattern. The skirt is not nearly as full as in the fashion plates and her hair and large bonnet are still much in the style of the 1840s. However, she has updated her appearance with her new fashioned hip-length fitted jacket with its lightly flared trumpet-shaped sleeves

21 A Welsh family 'burning the Guy', a rare view of winter outdoor dress photographed by John Dillwyn Llewellyn in 1851 and noted in his daughter's diary. The sisters wear the very popular tartan dresses and rather old-fashioned identical deep-crowned bonnets. The smallest girls, dressed the same, wear matching capes; the older girls shawls; that of the central girl has the elongated pine pattern border characteristic of the period, contrast coloured reserves and fringed border. It is probably square and would be folded diagonally in wear. The oldest lady has a smaller, more up-to-date bonnet and a triangular and possibly wadded fringe-trimmed mantle. Her skirts are of conventional indoor length, touching the ground at the back. The lad in the centre has a hip-length frock coat with flapped pockets and metal buttons, the little boy a short jacket Eton suit. Both they and the older man wear peaked caps

22 A study of two young ladies at a country door, a salt print taken by John Whistler in Hampshire in the early 1850s. Though well and even fashionably dressed, for the hairdressing and trumpet-shaped sleeves are conventional for the date, the girls lack the studied smartness assumed by sitters for the conventional portrait sitting. The inserted 'chemisette' in the front opening of the dress, the contrasting inner cuffs and the neck ribbons are the kind of accessory more common in life than in the fashion plate.

23 A contrast in coiffure. The girl on the left wears the 'bare faced' style with the hair puffed up at the forehead and pulled away from the face (a style popularised by the Empress Eugenie in 1853), complete with pseudo-Spanish curls. Her companion retains the dangling curls fashionable since the 1840s, and still popular with younger women for evening wear.

24 A lady of 1856, her dress typical with its horizontal emphasis, cuffs flaring from midway between elbow and shoulder, and full skirt with its pattern woven flounces. Her small bonnet is worn tilted away from the brow, allowing a good view of her hairstyle which dresses smoothly away from the centre parting and half covers her ears

25 Mrs Waterlow senior photographed by her son in 1856. She wears a fashionable lace mantle with frilled border and an equally up-to-date indoor cap worn well back with a wealth of decoration at the sides; less than justice is done to it by her hairstyle with its Regency-style curls, possibly additions made from crimped horsehair!

Opposite
26 A stereoscopic sequence of Victorian high life as purveyed to parlour viewers in the 1850s. In this 'At the Ball' it is possible to see that as in the 1840s the dresses are low-cut, but the waists are shorter and round and the wide well supported skirts copiously flounce-trimmed. Materials were light and gauzy and fire a constant hazard. Hair is dressed away from the face with floral wreaths arranged around the crown of the head. Fans have not changed in style since the late 1840s. Bouquets in decorative metal holders were another

popular ballroom accessory. The men wear full evening dress differing only in details of cut from that of today, and made from smooth-faced cloth, with black being the preferred colour; their stiff starched shirt fronts gleam above their low-cut waistcoats. Both black and white ties are worn, but by the later 1860s white only are permissible. For dancing, men wore flat glacé pumps and white kid gloves

Opposite

27 The younger lady of the Hayball family of Sheffield photographed by Arthur Hayball in the later 1850s has accepted the new fashions with elegance and poise. Her wide skirt floats supported by an adequate number of petticoats, either starched or crinoline reinforced and her fringe-trimmed mantle flows loosely. Her pretty flower and lace-trimmed bonnet is tipped far back on her neat little head, though it would have looked better in profile if she had also updated her hairstyle and pulled it back from her face. The lady standing at the back wears a bonnet, equally fashionable but at the wrong angle, being tilted too far forward, and her flounced dress needs but does not get enough petticoat support. However, she has at least tried to keep up with fashion, unlike her neighbour whose dress is too light in colour to register on the plate. This is perhaps as well, because her narrow skirts and low dressed hair are definitely those of the previous decade. The men are pillars of respectability in their tall 'chimney pot' hats, medium-high collars and wide flaring ties. The little girls wear easy fitting knee-length dresses, legs decently covered with calf-length drawers and light stockings. Shoes are square-toed and fasten with ankle bands

Above right

28 The actress Celeste Elliott wears a most elaborate evening toilette for her formal portrait in the late 1850s. It is made from moire trimmed with lace and bands of ruched ribbon. The triangular front panel and the three-dimensional trimming recall the Louis Quinze fashions which returned to favour a hundred years after their original inception. The 'bare faced' style is very typical of the mid-1850s, and the high-poised floral diadem echoes the line of the fashionable bonnet. She also wears patterned lace mittens.

29 Amy Sedgewick, the actress in the height or rather in the breadth of fashion, in the later 1850s. The square neck and ruched trim of her formal day dress suggest a return to the rococo, already recalled in the dress worn by Celeste Elliott (28)

30 Short skirts, sporty, sexy and smart. 'Beautiful May', 1858–60, an unusual, informal, outdoor portrait of a girl in a short simple walking dress supported well away from the legs (which the tactful amateur photographer has managed to leave in decent obscurity) by a crinoline. Many women found that in relieving them from heavy clinging petticoats, crinolines contributed greatly to their mobility and comfort. With it she wears an informal flat-crowned hat (a children's style which had only recently become acceptable for adults) and a light shawl

31 A more sophisticated lady pedestrian, *circa* 1860, her extrovert and ambivalent sexuality emphasised by her gaudily bejewelled tightly-waisted coat modelled on that of an eighteenth-century gentleman. Her skirts are festooned up – probably with internal pulley rings and tapes – to show her decorative underpetticoat; but still no legs!

32 This group of the Misses Spiller in 1858 allows a good view of a typical hairstyle of the late 1850s and early 1860s; drawn back to cover the ears. The lady to the right front shows well a widely worn style with a long rolled curl, giving the necessary fullness at the temple

33 Lady Elizabeth Adeane in a possibly Paisley woven shawl, photographed in 1858–60. Both her small, off-the-face bonnet and the elongated pine pattern on the shawl are fashionable for the date. Very long 'plaid' size shawls of this kind were doubled and then folded over at the top for extra warmth

34 Riding habits of the 1860s are looser and more comfortable than they had been earlier in Victoria's reign. In this photograph, taken 1858–60, Miss Fitton wears a high necked but hip-length close-buttoned jacket and full skirt, the length graduated to allow for even hang when mounted. Except for hunting, hats are the same as those worn for other informal occasions, and in this instance is a wide brimmed straw

35 The ladies in this group on the new jetty at Margate in about 1860 wear crinoline-supported skirts at their widest. Fortunately it is a calm day since, as contemporary caricaturists were so fond of illustrating, such skirts very quickly became unmanageable. The hat and sealskin-type mantle of the central lady are in the very latest fashion. The men wear walking dress with loose-cut low-waisted coats and full-cut trousers in contrasting colours and textures. The top hat became steadily lower in the mid-1860s but these should be compared with that in figure 179

36, 37 and **38** Girls dressing, from stereoscopic views of the early 1860s, possibly intended for a marginally pornographic market. In the first the girls can be seen in their hip-length corsets, worn over low-cut chemises and knee-length petticoats below which can be seen the lace of their drawers. These were garments which only came into general use at this period and the reason can be seen in the second view which shows a girl in a cage crinoline, which tended to sway revealingly. Similar skirt supports were introduced in the later 1850s and by 1860 had reached their largest size, though perhaps never quite the size of the exaggeratedly expansive example in figure 37. The average size skirt of the period is that worn by the maid. Under the crinoline is a long white petticoat and another would have been worn over it. Note that the corset laces at the back. The size and sway of the cage crinoline made it a good subject for comedy, and the comic stereo in figure 38 has many parellels in graphic art of the period

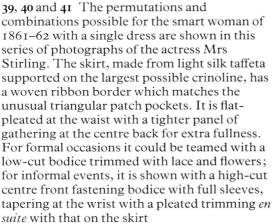

39, **40** and **41** The permutations and
combinations possible for the smart woman of
1861–62 with a single dress are shown in this
series of photographs of the actress Mrs
Stirling. The skirt, made from light silk taffeta
supported on the largest possible crinoline, has
a woven ribbon border which matches the
unusual triangular patch pockets. It is flat-
pleated at the waist with a tighter panel of
gathering at the centre back for extra fullness.
For formal occasions it could be teamed with a
low-cut bodice trimmed with lace and flowers;
for informal events, it is shown with a high-cut
centre front fastening bodice with full sleeves,
tapering at the wrist with a pleated trimming *en
suite* with that on the skirt

42 Lydia Thompson posed for her theatre publicity photograph *circa* 1860 in outdoor dress, a winter carriage mantle, somewhat oddly accessoried with a parasol. Travelling could be a chilly business in the mid-nineteenth century as carriages and trains were unheated, and quilted, caped and hooded mantles of the type popularised in the early nineteenth century remained in use, if not in fashion, until its end. The smooth sweeping lines make this as fashionable for its period as it was useful

43 An elderly lady *circa* 1860, wears a formal indoor dress. The width of her sleeves, which are in the latest fashion and flare from the armseye, is emphasised by a contrast coloured gathered trimming. It is made from moire, a stiff silk with a subtle watered pattern; this was much used for 'best dresses' and was very popular with photographers. The lady, elegant and expensively dressed as she is, still retains the smooth ear covering styles of her prime, 20 years before, underneath her pretty lace and ribbon-trimmed cap. Her heavy neck chain is characteristic of the date

44 Lady Hawarden's daughters assume a fashion-plate-like pose for their mother on a balcony in Kensington in about 1862. The girl on the left wears a semi-formal bonnet perched high on her head, and a shaped silk mantle on her wide, well supported skirt. Her sister, in an informal light spotted dress, wears a pretty 'Tyrolean' type hat and appears, from the dangling folds of her hem, to have removed her crinoline, the support of which might have made her dress too wide for the focal length of the lens

45 A young lady of 1862 in a simple polka dot summer dress with the fashionably full 'Bishop' sleeve and a triangular 'Swiss' belt. Belts and sashes were a popular way of defining the fashionable angular silhouette without recourse to tight corseting. Her coiffure is equally up-to-date, the fullness built out at the temples in a series of roll curls

46 Another informal summer mantle, this time completely of machine-made lace, an accessory of which this provincial lady *circa* 1860 was obviously very proud. The fullness of the skirts made it essential for upper garments to flow without restriction

47 For their engagement picture in 1862 Princess Alexandra of Denmark and Albert Prince of Wales wear informal dress such as would have been conventional for any young couple in the kingdom. The Prince wears a velvet lounge jacket and check trousers, and the Princess a loose jacket over her crinoline-supported geometric patterned skirt with its angular Greek key pattern braid trimming. The fold marks, clearly visible, are something of a prestige status, symbols with a long tradition especially in continental portraiture, and imply a pristine new garment. The short jacket she wears is probably a 'zouave', modelled more or less after the Greek original with hanging sleeves. She was fond of such accessories, explaining to her future mother in law, Queen Victoria, that they made it possible to combine variety with economy – an essential for anyone, especially a Princess with a small dress allowance. It was an example that many girls found useful, particularly when skirts used so much material. She wears her hair smoothly drawn back from the face, the coils secured in one of the very popular nets or 'snoods'

48 Princess Alexandra's beauty and popularity made whatever she wore a model for millions of Englishwomen of all classes. In another of her commemorative engagement portraits in 1862, she wears a summer mantle, unwaisted and flared with wide-cut sleeves. Cashmere or an easily washable wool and cotton mixture would have been a popular contemporary choice, together with trimming of applied bands of machine-made lace. She carries a youthful, informal, flat-crowned hat and a tightly rolled umbrella

49 Alexandra of Denmark and Albert Edward Prince of Wales were married on 10 March 1863 at St George's Chapel, Windsor. The Prince wore the blue and ermine robes of a Knight of the Garter over the scarlet black and gold uniform of a general in the army. The bride wore white satin which, according to the *Illustrated London News* was 'trimmed with chatelaines of orange blossoms, myrtle and bouffants of tulle with Honiton lace; the train of silver moire antique' similarly trimmed. The dress was made by Mrs James of London and may have been paid for by the King of the Belgians. He had wanted to give the bride a Worth dress but political considerations prevailed. This is one of the formal commemorative photographs issued for the wedding. It was taken by Mayall and is sometimes, quite often colourfully, retouched

50 Contrast trimming was very popular in the 1860s and was sometimes achieved with applied decoration. This was greatly facilitated by the use of the sewing machine, which became widespread in the late 1850s. This dress worn by a girl of the early 1860s uses applied braid rondels to suggest the line of the very popular 'Bolero' jacket and waistcoat

1865–1879

51 Jane Burden (Mrs William Morris), the pre-Raphaelite painter Dante Gabriel Rossetti's favourite model, was posed by him in 1865 for a set of photographs by Maynard which were to be pictorial references for his painting. Mrs Morris and other ladies of similar tastes found the corset and crinolines of mid-Victorian England totally unaesthetic and devised their own 'picturesque' attire. Significantly, the fashionable of the second half of the decade would endorse their choice, and in dropping out of the mode in this plain, loose-cut dress with its medium-full flowing skirt with embroidered collar and cuffs, Mrs Morris is not denying fashion so much as anticipating it

52, **53** and **54** The practice of wearing mourning clothes was formalised and if possible intensified after the death of the Prince Consort in 1861. The successful London drapers, Peter Robinson, opened a new shop in Regent Street in 1865 to concentrate on this branch of the trade and publicised it with what seems to be the first ever photographically illustrated clothes catalogue, from which these prints are taken.

The window display is typical for the date. Figure 52 shows the stark and enveloping outfit considered suitable for a widow with its veil, coif-like cap and cloak. The bonnets exploit the decorative possibilities, especially of jet trimming, permissible when the first intense period of mourning had passed. Black is not easy to photograph and the quality of these photographs would be exceptional even today

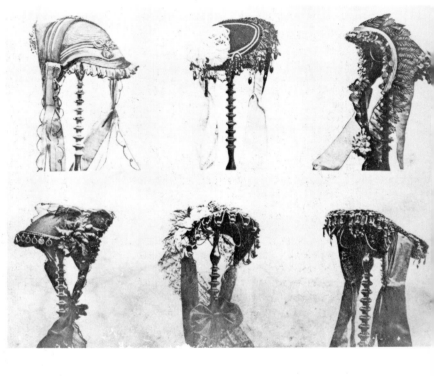

55 Mrs Grant, photographed by Silvy in 1866, exploits to the full the decorative potential of contrasts of texture in her velvet and ruched tulle full evening dress. The overdress looks forward to those of the 1870s, and it is interesting to compare it with the dress worn by Celeste Elliott (28), as characteristic of the preceding silhouette. Notice also her jewellery

56 The more severe and angular style characteristic of the second half of the decade is well illustrated by this photograph of Marie Wilton in *Ours*, produced in 1866. The vertical stripe emphasises the way the skirt is gored, so that it flares without undue fullness. She wears a tip-tilted hat and carries a black lace shawl and a rather sleek parasol

57 A closer look at the coiffure of the mid-1860s is provided by this clever double image photograph of the actress Mrs Bandmann Palmer, possibly by Silvy. There is fullness at the temples, provided by close set waves, and the hair is then pulled back clear of the ears to be looped into a loose knot set low at the back of the head and anchored by a possibly false braid

Above right and right

58 and **59** Fashion of the mid-1860s – two full length views, the chic in figure 58, the clumsy in figure 59. After reaching their greatest size in about 1860, skirts began rapidly to diminish (at least for day occasions), and crinolines when worn also became smaller. The dire consequences of economy are well shown in figure 59; in wearing last year's foundation garments under this year's clothes, the crinoline is seen to be too big and the corset too small. Apart from this there is little to distinguish the two ladies, at least as far as style goes. Both dresses have epaulets on the rather full but tapering sleeves, and a short waist emphasised by a belt. The decoration on the dress in figure 58 is probably tatted – a technique introduced in the 1840s. Note also the long watch guard and brooch in figure 59

60 and **61** Elena di Murska, a dramatic soprano of mysterious Hungarian origin, swept flamboyantly across the opera world in the second half of the 1860s, making her London debut in 1865. An abundance of hair was a much coveted attribute in the late 1860s, and she was almost as famous for the luxuriance of her locks (usually, though enviously, conceded to be all her own), as for the beauty of her voice and her tumultuous private life. Her skirt has the angular trimming and back emphasis which became fashionable at this time; in figure 60 she wears a day bodice, in figure 61 the low-cut formal version

62 The short walking skirt is worn in this photograph by Princess Alexandra, seen with Prince Victor and Prince George in 1868. There was considerable contemporary controversy about the decency or otherwise of short skirts (that is, above the ankle), but this very smart example, with its loose sack jacket and Hussar braid trim, must have done a great deal to make the style acceptable

63 An unusual informal domestic group, 'Mother and Sister Marie', dated 1868, provides an intimate view of the essentials of average middle-class dress towards the end of the decade. The dresses are plain, contrast trimmed, and the skirts flared rather than full, with a more tightly gathered panel at the centre back waist. Sister Marie's hairstyle has already been explained in the caption to figure 57 while 'mother' has hers rolled high and away from the face. The long strands at the back are looped into a bun; in a close up photograph from the same series this is shown to have been kept tidy with a hair net

Opposite

64 A couple photographed in Newcastle in the later 1860s wearing informal walking dress: he in a double-breasted reefer suit and flat bowler and she in a dress which combines the wide sleeve more characteristic of the early 1860s with the gathered drapes and peplum which were to be developed and formalised in the 1870s. Her pork pie hat is trimmed at the back with the long ribbons known to contemporaries as 'Follow me lads'

65 An informal portrait of an unknown but
seemingly very upper class family grouped in a
corner of a formal garden in the late 1860s. The
gentlemen provide a good conspectus of High
Victorian age and profession. The oldest,
seated centre, wears a dark formal morning suit
with skirts turned up over his knees to avoid
possible creasing and a tall top hat in the style
of the previous decade. It should be compared
with the much lower top hat carried by the
gentleman with the velvet lounge jacket and
waistcoat teamed with trousers decorated with
a contrast stripe on the seam. The youngest
man wears a light lounge suit and carries the
new fashion cut down top hat cum bowler
sometimes known as the 'Muller cut down' (see
figure 186). His hairstyle is fashionable and the
centre parting and side quiffs recall the
contemporary ladies' coiffure. On the opposite
side of the arch stands a clergyman in full loose
clerical frock coat with high collar and white
cravat. The oldest lady wears a goffered
(gathered) widow's cap of which there is a
closer view in figure 149. The young lady to
the left of the arch is dressed in a contrast
coloured skirt and blouse, the latter a garment
which became very popular for informal
occasions in the later 1860s. Her skirt should
be compared with that in figure 64. The three
little girls, probably sisters, wear identical
contrast-trimmed and scallop-edged frocks.
The two older girls (their cousins?) wear their
hair long and have identical striped frocks.

66 and **67** By 1868, the date this girl sat for her photograph in Dumfries, back fullness on a straight slightly flared skirt had just begun to be fashionable. Here it is provided by the addition of a small peplum. Her hair, piled high over the brow with the back in long ringlets, confirms her very fashionable appearance. Its inspiration was the complex coiffure of late 'Louis Seize', an epoch which a century later was to seem very attractive to the fashionables of the 1870s. For the other view

(67), probably from the same sitting, the girl has changed to outdoor mantle and short walking-length skirt. Her stance is almost a deportment book illustration of the 'Grecian bend' so often caricatured at the time. The diagonal line from tip-tilted brow clinging hat to backward thrusting bustle is emphasised by her neat but substantial umbrella, which was probably called into occasional use to support her in the newly introduced, fashionable and very high-heeled shoes

68 and **69** Miss Clifton has her hair dressed in the latest fashion for her photograph by Elliott and Fry in 1868. As in figure 66 her coiffure aspires to the height and elaboration of the styles of the third quarter of the eighteenth century, achieved by topping a high coronet of plaited braids with a mass of loose curls. Any or all of this may well have been false, for this was the great period of false hair, as the early photographic advertisement of 1872 illustrates (69). The soft edged trimming of her dress, heavy lace cuffs and pleated gauze are essential features of the fashions of the time

70 Mother seems to have worn an old dress for this Liverpool family photograph of the very late 1860s and is probably similar in class and attitude to the lady in figure 58. Her daughter is much more up to date with her peplum overskirt, jabot and high-piled chignon – all features which were to carry over into the 1870s. A comparison between the styles worn by mother and daughter explains why dresses of the late 1860s are so rare in museum collections; provided with additional overskirts and rather more bouncy trimming they could carry on in wear for several more years

71 and 72 This unknown Rochdale lady (71) *circa* 1870, has succeeded very well in her arrangement of the dense high-piled chignon characteristic of the late 1860s and early 1870s. As the portrait of the actress Fanny Brough illustrates (72), styles of this complexity required hats of different shape and worn at a new angle, flat on the crown of the head

73 and **74** Semi-formal gowns of 1872. Lady
O'Hagan, new wife of the Lord Chancellor of
Ireland, wears a conventional evening dress
with a lace-edged velvet bodice and draped
overskirt over trained and deeply flounced
taffeta (73); this emphasises the fashionable
tipped forward stance dictated by the large
bustle and by the way she leans on the
photographer's decorative plinth. Her fan,
with its shaped fabric leaves, is interesting, as
is the large decorative crucifix at her neck. The
1870s were a period when religion – and its
appurtenances – was a very live issue.

Teresa Furtado, the burlesque artist, wears a
dress of similar cut, but raised to high fashion
by its choice of material, a silk in one of the
small figured 'Louis Seize' designs, and by its
velvet banded lace overskirt (74). Her hairstyle
is altogether a more complex and professional
construction than Lady O'Hagan's coiffure,
though the shape is the same

75 By 1874, the date of this formal studio portrait of Mrs Brealey by Elliott and Fry, the fashionable line had become straighter and more severe. Bustles were still worn, but they were smaller. The waist is beginning to lengthen and sleeves are much less wide. Velvet bands and regular machine pleating make the effect much heavier than the fluffy edges previously popular for decoration. The use of the machine and all the other mechanical devices patented to make the dressmaker's life easier resulted in an increased but regular and regimented elaboration of effect

76 Ada Cavendish, the actress, photographed *circa* 1870 in smart day dress, illustrating the alternative inspiration, the 'washerwoman skirt' with the overdress pulled high and draped back. Her dress is walking length, well clear of the ground. Pleating, machine tucked and stitched, was to be a fashion feature of the last quarter of the century. She wears, on her copious coiffure, one of the new 'postillion' hats

Opposite
77 Miss Millar wears a dress in the very latest fashion for this portrait study by Elliott and Fry in 1875. It retains the bustle and train but is comparatively straight in front. Colour contrast and the intricately ruched front emphasise the slim silhouette. Her hair is still piled high on the crown, but the slight fringe and lower chignon suggest that a change of style is imminent

78 Adelina Patti was only slightly less famous for her beauty and dress sense than she was for her singing. At this period she patronised the Paris couturier Worth and in the photograph, taken *circa* 1875, she wears a dress with the new fashionable straighter skirt drawn back into a low set bustle and train. The line is much more figure defining and harder edged, though here it is softened as well as emphasised by bands of artificial flowers

79 Mme Thea was photographed in skating dress of fur-trimmed cloth by Nadar in 1876, the wintry atmosphere being increased by spotting the plate to give the effect of snow. Despite the dubious practicality of the style with its 'tied-back' skirt so tightly drawn as not to need the support of a bustle, the hobble effect only marginally modified by the kilted underskirt, the very tightly fitting jacket and the precariously balanced feather-trimmed hat, it was considered suitable for engraved reproduction as a fashion plate in the *Englishwoman's Magazine* of 1876, and paper patterns were available at a not inexpensive 5s 6d each

80 and **81** Fashion and dress, or the ideal and the reality! Lillie Langtry (80), launched herself on a career as popular pin-up almost immediately after her triumphant entry into High Victorian society in 1876. She had made her successful first impression in a plain black dress, but as soon as her means permitted she deserted her little Jersey dressmaker for the French couture. In this photograph *circa* 1878 by Downey, to whom she first syndicated her image, she wears a day dress of exceptional elegance, a tightly fitted sheath, the essentials of her notably seductive shape framed in most effective *trompe l'oeil* velvet bands. This was obviously an example to be followed, as the unknown lady in figure 81 illustrates. It was not an easy time for the plump, as corseting was rigid, the line – or in this case, the lines – uncompromising, and fans, though larger than they had been in the second quarter of the century, still not quite big enough. It might have been a little better if she had also adopted Lillie's hairstyle, for the severity of the style needed the softening effect of the fashionable fringe

82 and **83** An evening dress of 1876 as worn by Mary Eykin, a Northamptonshire lady. The line is fashionably tight fitting, but hardly visible under its camouflage of striped ribbon, lace and artificial flowers. Nevertheless, if compared with the dress of 1875 shown in figure 77, it is possible to see how the line has tightened up. It is a pity that Mrs Eykin is reluctant to adopt the newly fashionable fringe, but we know from contemporary comments that the more conservative considered it made the wearer look like a poodle

84 Peter Robinson produced a photographic catalogue, their *Book of Styles*, in 1876, to launch a mail order ready-to-wear department. From the few surviving examples it would seem that they used the *carte de visite* form and put details, prices and descriptions on the back. The text which accompanied the picture, printed on the reverse reads: 'This silk costume, price complete 5½ guineas is made of Rich Lyons Gros Grain . . . in any color, or two shades combined, also in Black or Black and White Check as represented. Patterns of the Silk and forms for self-measurement sent by post'

85 Evelyn Rayne, the young English musical comedy actress, was photographed in the late 1870s wearing a conventional summer outfit. The tied back line was modified for more active pursuits into a hip-length bodice with sash border and a pleated skirt, and in this form was also worn by little girls. Her hat is worn straight and reveals a neat chignon at the back and a fringe in front

86 By 1878 the fashionable line had become elongated and very slender indeed, and Princess line dresses, called perhaps after Princess Alexandra, with no waist seams at all, had become popular. In this view of Miss Brewer from the Elliott and Fry collection and dated 1878, she wears a severe all-in-one piece dress with gauged front panel. Her single accessory is a fashionable large and heavy fan attached to a cord girdle. Her unknown companion wears a formal frock coat with natural waist and trousers which flare slightly over his boots

87 Another view of the Princess line dress of 1878, here worn by Miss Brierley and an unknown friend. Comparing this profile view with that of Mary Eykin in figure 82 (dated 1876), it can be seen how in the space of two years the fullness of the skirt, unsupported by any form of bustle, has now slipped from back waist to hip. The ladies are posed, rather improbably, given the length and complexity of their trains, in front of the Elliott and Fry stock beach set. Miss Brierley – if she is the foremost lady – wears a Tyrolean hat, and her companion one of ruched satin. Hats are still worn almost flat, tilted slightly forward to accommodate the now rather small chignon

75

88 In sympathy with the fashionable line of the late 1870s and 1880s riding habits were made much more tightly fitting. Mrs Watney posed for her 1878 studio portrait by Elliott and Fry in a correct formal riding dress. It has the necessarily long skirt, the desired smooth line being achieved by having the fullness gored rather than gathered, and a close-buttoned, high-collared jacket to the snug fit of which tailors devoted a great deal of attention. It is short with a graduated basque, echoing in miniature the shape of the man's tail coat. The stiff cuffs with their flamboyant cuff links are another masculine touch, as is the tip-tilted top hat – though this is feminised with a wisp of tulle

1880–1900

Below

89 The Jersey Lily's style was followed in hats as well as in other forms of dress. This unknown follower of fashion, around 1880, wears a hat copied from one of her soft draped toques. The cuirasse bodice is exceptionally well made and fitted and she carries one of the new fashioned, rather large and heavy parasols with knob handle and lace frilled edge. Note also the above wrist-length gloves which usually accompany the shorter tighter sleeve between 1876 and the 1880s

90 Sarah Bernhardt was another celebrity whose very considerable publicity emphasised clothes and life style only slightly less than her acting ability. She was notorious, at least among the French couture, for the way in which she shared out her patronage, but it seems likely that the dress in which she was photographed by Sarony during her American tour in 1880 was from Worth, a house which at this period was making stark straight dresses, their severity relieved only by the magnificent large patterned silks. The combination of high collar, short sleeve and long gloves would have been considered rather daring by contemporaries, but they would be undeniably effective for someone of Sarah Bernhardt's unusual grace and slimness

91 Mrs Wright was photographed in winter walking dress in 1880. It is instructive to compare her with Mme Thea (79) who had been photographed in a similar gown and pose only four years earlier. The differences are subtle; the waistline is slightly shorter and the skirt hangs straight, no longer being pulled tight to the figure by a back drape, but with its fullness again supported by a bustle. The sleeves are higher set and the bonnet worn tilted back rather than over the forehead.

Opposite

92 and **93** The decoration on Mrs Mackenzie's dress in her photograph of 1881 (92) emphasises the main features of dress at this date. She wears a corset-like 'cuirasse' bodice with an almost cache-sexe type of overskirt. Her legs are bound and hobbled, and her décolletage veiled rather than concealed by heavy net, the whole rather belatedly, perhaps, sanctified by a crucifix. The salient portions of this delectable package are emphasised by fashionably heavy beaded trimming. More discriminating contemporaries commented on the considerable, though covert, sexuality of the style, but they tended to be French. The English were less concerned with its moral than its physical consequences – the length and tightness of the corset (Mrs Mackenzie's bulges above and below are quite evident) – and the restriction of movement caused by the very tight sleeves, the skirt and the weight of the train.

Contemporary critics had little effect on the average Englishwoman; the unknown Kensington lady (93) has done her best to follow a fashionable example by using the by now widely available home dressmaking paper pattern. She has managed the fit of the bodice, which clings with corset – rather than figure – hugging tightness, and used another pattern for the skirt. Very similar designs were advertised in R. Munroe, *Practical Dressmaking*, 1879

94 Lillie Langtry entered the acting profession in 1882. Her beauty had matured since her entry into society in 1877 and she has changed her hairstyle, dressing it in the height of contemporary fashion with a soft curled fringe and a small chignon at the nape of the neck

Below left

95 By 1885, for her appearance in *Peril*, she has changed her hairstyle in accordance with the mode, which is for a smaller, neater, closer to the head coiffure. She retains her fringe, but the back hair is coiled on the crown and not knotted at the nape. She carries a new fashioned large ostrich feather fan. The lines of her bustle are perhaps a little too visible under her plain satin train. Note also the short waist and the high shoulder line, all characteristic of 1880s fashion

Opposite

96 A family group of the early 1880s, showing how cumbersome styles of the period were adapted to daily wear, with lightweight tops, almost like belted blouses, being worn with pleated skirts, a combination which permits considerable freedom of movement. It is a style adaptable for young and old. The lady third from the right and wearing the more restrictive fashionable style, points the contrast. The indoor cap of the elderly and those of the children are styled like the hats of the period. The frilly yet heavy parasol is characteristic of the 1880s

97 Summer dresses of the mid-1880s, made from simple striped washing fabric. The wearers may be sisters because the material is the same for both dresses though the style differs. The younger girl still wears her hair down, but the elder has hers coiled up in a bun. They are simple every day dresses of their time with high band collars and draped and gathered bustles

98 Lady Ramos Mexia is gowned in the height of fashion for her 1884 photograph. Her formal day dress, made from rich flower patterned silk damask, has the predictably large bustle, but the sleeves have a puff at the shoulder instead of being smoothly set. This is a feature which was advocated in England by the dress reformers and in Paris by only the most advanced of the couturiers. From her elegance it would seem that the latter influence dominated, though Elliott and Fry's rather oriental bric-a-brac might suggest that they shopped at East India House. Arthur Liberty had opened a shop in 1875, which was just beginning to make a name for itself as the purveyor of aesthetic and rational dress for the advanced woman, as well as for fancy goods in the Eastern mode

99 Women were becoming more active and intellectual in the 1880s, and in sympathy with these hitherto masculine tastes developed a preference for plain tailor modes often in fabrics which had previously been confined to men's suits. This lady, photographed 1884–85, wears a trim check wool bodice and skirt. Her bustle, reintroduced at the beginning of the decade to support the dragging weight of the skirt, is as feminine as her neat, starched, stud-fastening cuffs are masculine

100 As this photograph of the actress Ellen Terry shows, partial relief for those constrained by the fashions of the mid-1880s was obtained by wearing an informal 'tea-gown' so called because it was intended to be worn at around five o'clock before a lady changed into formal clothes for dinner. It was often, as here, in the form of an overdress and a loose undertunic which, unwaisted, did not need to be worn over a corset. Ellen Terry, though fashion conscious, was unconventional and preferred the less fitting lines of clothes advocated by the Dress Reform Movement

101 Violet Cameron, the musical comedy star, was photographed in the mid-1880s in a tailored jacket with matching waistcoat which she wears with a rounded ladylike bustle-supported skirt. She carries one of the fashionably large parasols and wears the wrist-length gloves conventional at this date. Another print shows that her hair is arranged in the style which was to become popular at the end of the decade, dressed very close to the head and with the back arranged in a French pleat held by a comb on the short curly cut crown and which can be seen (110) worn by Madame Patti. Her hat, worn straight, is small, with vertical emphasis provided by a trimming of at least half a dead bird. Such trimmings became so popular at this period that a few species, such as the very luxuriantly feathered grebe, were almost rendered extinct

102 Miss E. Shepherd in full court dress photographed by Elliott and Fry in 1885. The three feathers, the veil and bouquet, as well as the low-cut decolletage, are *de rigeur* for her presentation as debutante and are worn with full evening dress in white and with train of regulation length

103 It is left to an unknown Guildford girl to provide an illustration of quintessential outdoor fashion for the mid-1880s. She wears a well fitted tailor-made coat with a very smart, tall, ribbon-trimmed hat worn at the correct fashionable angle, high on the crown of the head. She carries a long fur boa and an astrakhan purse muff

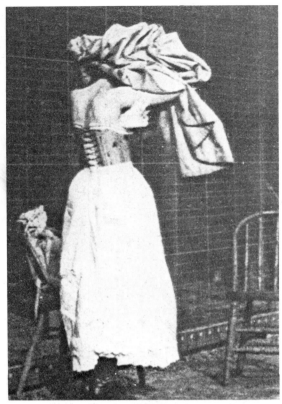

104, 105 and **106** Dressing and undressing in late Victorian times as recorded by Eadweard Muybridge in his *Figures in Motion* published between 1883 and 1887. The illustrations have been put together from plates 423 and 494. The basic garment is a low-necked sleeveless calf length linen or cotton chemise. Over this come straight knee-length drawers, trimmed at the knee, with the chemise pulled through the back opening to provide extra support for the back of the dress in lieu of the bustle. The corset, sometimes coloured, adjusts for size by lacing at the back and fastens with hooks at the front. It is hip-length and closely boned in order to support the bust and compress the waist. Over this is worn a just below knee-length dark, probably silk, petticoat, and then a fuller flounced white one to give the proper flowing line to the dress skirt. The stockings, already on before the picture sequence begins, are supported above the knee with garters and have a fancy band at boot top level

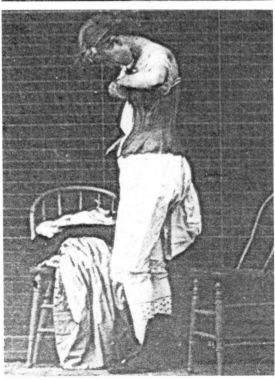

108 Despite mounting criticism mourning conventions were still rigorously observed during the 1880s, the width and number of the crepe bands conveying the duration and the degree of kinship. This unknown lady is in the very deepest mouring and has eschewed white even at neck and wrists. The only contrast in her attire is the cap, plain and round, and not the pointed 'Marie Stuart' shape which was sometimes worn

107 In the 1880s underwear began to be pretty rather than merely functional. Mlle Charmion, photographed in faintly naughty pose by the theatrical photographers Alfred Ellis and Walery, wears a ribbon-and-lace-trimmed chemise under her short, well boned corset and sleek fitted silk petticoat with decorative border. Underwear was usually white, though sometimes by the 1880s the smartest was made from coloured silk

109 Princess Alice of Hesse, Queen Victoria's grand-daughter, a mature and somewhat melancholy 16 year old, later to be Czarina of Russsia, sent this photograph to a friend in 1888. The dress she wears is a good illustration of the conventional line of the mid-1880s, with its close-fitting natural waist-length bodice and fairly wide, straight and pleated skirt, with the back fullness supported on a bustle. The vertical emphasis is confirmed by the small coiffure with hair piled on the crown and the high-set shoulder line. Unlike Lady Ramos Mexia and Ellen Terry, she has accepted the conventional discomfort of the straight tight sleeve

110 Madame Patti obtained this magnificent concert dress from the Paris couture house of Morin Blossier before taking herself and her 24 trunks on a triumphant tour of America in 1888. The photograph by Walery was engraved for *Woman's World* in the same year as part of her pre-concert publicity, where it is described as being made from 'net embroidered with forget-me-nots over a pink satin petticoat' and trimmed with 'cascades of velvet, roses and a sash of leaf green velvet'. She carries a fine example of one of the new fashioned feather fans

111 The clothes of the Scrope sisters span the range of middle-of-the-road fashion which could have been worn in the later 1880s. The two youngest girls are dressed in sheer fabrics, somewhat in the aesthetic style, with loose-cut, square-necked bodices, sashes and medium-full, though straight, skirts. The one standing to the left of the sundial displays a similar taste for the aesthetic in her mediaeval inspired gown with a preference for the pretty rather than the severe. Their hair is dressed close to the head. It is interesting to compare the longer-waisted styles of the older girls, perhaps wearing last year's dresses, with the more up-to-date short waists of the younger ones

112 The beautiful Lady Brooke wears a heavy brocaded mantle with a luxurious fox fur trim for this photograph published in *Men and Women of the Day* in 1889. At this period overgarments were almost invariably slit or shaped at the centre back to allow for the size of the bustle. Her hair is dressed with the curly fringe popularised by the Princess of Wales. Close set waves of this kind were easier to achieve after M. Marcel had perfected his technique of tong waving in the late 1870s

113 Mrs John Wood, the American actress, was included in *Men and Women of the Day*, 1889, but she preferred either a slightly out-of-date photograph or an old dress, because the style with its fairly long waist and asymmetric drape, short tight sleeve and heavy fur trimming was more characteristic of the first half of the decade

Above opposite

114 A family party of about 1890. The older man wears a suit with a cutaway line more characteristic of the late 1870s and the Dundrearies of his prime, 30 years previously. Beards like that of his companion were rare among Englishmen in the 1890s, but his suit is conventional enough. The little boys wear sailor suits with the obligatory long dark stockings. The young ladies are dressed in the height of fashion and their dresses have puffed sleeves and short waists marked by a sash or shaped belt, while their skirts are flared with the bustle now diminished to a mere pleat. Wide, flat-brimmed hats began to be fashionable in the late 1880s

Left

115 and **116** Alfred Ellis took this photograph
of Ada Blanche, the actress, in the early to mid-
1890s, wearing full evening dress of lace-
trimmed satin. The fashionable full sleeves
emphasise and diminish the size of the waist.
Ada Blanche sent this to an admirer who
cherished it; however, she was not quite slim
enough for the tastes of another fan, who
touched out the sides of her waist, giving her a
wholly unnatural slenderness. There are
instances of waists measuring even less than
the legendary norm of Victorian England, 18
inches, but these are exceptional, extraordinary
even, and the result of prolonged and
deliberate figure training. Retouching a
photograph was a much easier way of catering
for a minority taste, but such views were a not
unimportant part of a collector's market

Opposite

117 This dinner dress of about 1892 illustrates the change of fashionable emphasis from skirt to bodice where the width and height of the sleeve are stressed by contrast of colour, epaulets and applied trimming. Only a vestige of the bustle is left and the skirt fits smoothly over the hips. It is interesting to compare the length of the conventional waistline with the much higher level which the Empire line dress (119) attempted to popularise

118 Elaborate bodices were a feature of the fashions of the 1890s when the style emphasis shifted from the skirt to the sleeve. Florence St John, the musical comedy star, sent this charming photograph to a fan in 1899, but the full leg of mutton sleeves and dragonfly headdress are much more characteristic of the early and middle of the decade than the end

119 In the early 1890s there was an attempt to revive the modes of the First Empire, the element common to both periods being the large sleeve. Some evening dresses were made with high waists, but except for the aesthetically inclined it was a fashion more popular in France than in England, though high waists had a certain currency for informal 'tea gowns'. This magnificent large photograph was an exhibition piece by James Arthur

120 The Gaiety Girl or Cissie Fitzgerald hat publicised by the musical comedy of that name was first produced at the Prince of Wales Theatre in 1893 going on to become an enormous success in New York in 1895, where the fashion promotion which prompted this photograph took place. The hat is similar to several of its time in both England and the United States in having a low crown and a wide brim and feather trimming. Like most ladies' head gear in the middle and second half of the decade it was worn straight and high on the crown allowing for a large bun of hair just above the nape of the neck and puffed hair at the brow. Note also the caped collar and the leg-of-mutton sleeves so typical of the period. The photograph illustrates the ever increasing connection between stage and fashion publicity

121 Irene Vanbrugh in the mid-1890s, wearing a dress with the full sleeve so typical of the middle of the decade. It is shown with the waist-length cloak, the ubiquitous wrap of the period when sleeves had become so wide it was physically impossible to insert them into the armhole of any outer garment. By the middle of the decade skirts had become so widely flared it was feared that the crinoline would be introduced

122 Chelmsford Cycling Club members in the mid-1890s wear clothes typical for their age and date. The girls, all in fashionable full sleeves, wear blouses and/or jackets, full, flared skirts, collars and ties. Their boaters, perched straight on the crown of the head, are wider-brimmed than in the 1880s. There had been attempts to devise more specialised costumes with bloomers and divided skirts, but by the 1890s cycling had become so popular it was an ordinary everyday pursuit rather than a specialised sport, while with the improved safety bicycle, a slight shortening of the skirt was all that was necessary. The men wear tweed knickerbocker suits

123 Informal dress of 1897 worn by Lady Stone, wife of Sir Benjamin, who took the photograph, Mrs Derry, and friends at Studley Castle, Warwickshire. The girls wear blouses with fashionably full sleeves, neatly belted into wide, flared skirts which had replaced the straighter semi-bustled line in about 1895. Straw boaters and cravats were a popular unisex accessory. Lady Stone is dressed in the height of fashion in a dress, with sleeves which are just beginning to become smaller. It has only a small puff at the shoulders and a wide flared skirt

124 Mrs Charles Flower of Avonbank near Stratford in 1899 wears a braided hip-length cloak and a flared, velvet-banded skirt, accessoried with a fox fur and a small feather-trimmed hat. Mrs Flower is dressed fashionably, but similar clothes were to be worn by ladies of a certain age well into the next century. Bonnets were now worn only by the elderly

125 and **126** Simple, adaptable, semi-tailored informal clothes were popular with many ladies now leading a more active existence at the end of the nineteenth century. This Godmanchester lady wears one of the many popular matching outfits, consisting in this instance of a jacket, skirt and bodice with an optional high inserted collar, here worn with a shaped belt. It was dress or suit as desired. The sailor style bodice is aptly partnered by a straw boater, popular for summer wear from the mid-1880s. The hair begins to be dressed much more loosely from about 1894, and by the middle of the decade is so arranged that it half covered the ears

127 and **128** By the end of the decade the
fashionable line had become much smoother
and more flowing, and decoration emphasised
the new style 'S' bend figure moulded by the
straighter fronted corset. Irene Vanbrugh's
clothes in Pinero's comedy *The Gay Lord
Quex*, 1899, made by Messrs Jay of Regent
Street, aroused appreciative comment in the
press. In line with her new-style occupation
(she portrayed a manicurist, a profession
introduced from America in the early 1890s),
the clothes have an understated, up-to-date
elegance, as these publicity shots by Alfred
Ellis and Walery illustrate. Here she wears a
simple cloth day dress, the lines emphasised by
a minimal embroidered trimming, and the
severity modified by the soft cravat (127). For
visiting her clients she wears a tip tilted toque
and a hip-length fitted tailored jacket (128)

129 Irene, the gallant Irish manicurist in the
risqué comedy drama, *The Gay Lord Quex*,
1899, wears a kimono as a dressing gown,
perhaps one of the products of Liberty's
profitable promotion of goods from the East

130 For day, a soft effect was achieved with tucks and insertion. A photograph of about 1900 by James Arthur illustrates the woman of the new century with her swan-like silhouette, whose shape is achieved by a straight-fronted corset, the aim of which was to support the waist without compression. The waistline is lower, curving downwards, the bodice softly draped and the sleeves smoothly fitting with only a band of embroidery to recall the fullness fashionable until the very end of the 1890s. The skirt is gored and cross cut to flow smoothly from hip to ground, and with only a slight fullness at the back to recall the bustle

131 By 1900, 'La Ligne', the smooth flowing silhouette, had triumphed over the puffed sleeve and flared skirt of the middle of the decade. This lady's problems with the new silhouette were solved by some fairly heavy retouching, signs still faintly visible down her front! The ideal was an understated opulence emphasised by pale colours and fragile decoration, as in this dress whose sheer fabric is embroidered with sequins and trimmed with artificial flowers. The hair of this unknown but very elegant model, an exhibition photograph by James Arthur, is puffed out at the temples, anticipating the wide dressed, loosely waved coiffure of the Edwardian period

Children's Dress

132 and **133** The Fox Talbot children aged a
few weeks, three, five and seven years, when
Fox Talbot took their photographs on 5 and 19
April 1842, marking the date on the corner of
the print. The weather must have changed
rapidly, for in the first the children wear winter
dress and in the second summer clothes. As in
most respectable families, the sisters are
dressed alike, for winter in fur-trimmed velvet
and for summer in print with a lace or
embroidery trim. They do not change their
bonnets, deep-brimmed, ribbon-trimmed
straws. The clarity of the second picture is
such that it is possible to see that the children's
dresses are low necked and short sleeved with
additional capes and extra sleeves to bridge any
chilly gaps, and that stockings are light and
shoes have ankle bands. The Fox Talbots seem
a rather old-fashioned family; the high-waisted
scant-skirted dresses look back to the '30s and
do not have the conventional full skirted look
of the '40s. These are very early photographs,
and it seems that the adults had not yet
appreciated the necessity of remaining still, for
there is a double image of the deep bonnet and
indoor cap (132)

134 Master Grierson, photographed in Edinburgh, *circa* 1844, wearing a light tunic jacket trimmed with military-style rows of buttons and having a deep, gently pleated skirt. His wide straight trousers look as though they match, and the tucks in the hem would allow for growth. His shoes are flat-heeled and square-toed with a ribbon bow on the high-cut vamp. He wears a neckerchief – perhaps because Hill and Adamson were attempting to secure a moderate colour contrast – for it was more usual to fold the shirt collar over the neckline of the tunic. He carries a high-crowned, deep-brimmed, coarsely woven summer straw hat

135 Two small girls of the early 1850s wearing the kind of fashionable dress disliked by the dress reformers because of the low-cut, chilly and restrictive bodices. The clarity of the daguerreotype, which may be American, is such that it provides uncensored and uncompromising comment on the neat lively little images of the fashion plate child

136 In 1857, the Royal Family posed informally on the terrace at Osborne to celebrate the birth of the latest and last addition, the Princess Beatrice, seen here in long gown and caped carrying cloak in Queen Victoria's arms. The Queen herself wears informal outdoor dress, a gathered bonnet at the fashionable angle well off the forehead, and a loose, light cape. The Prince Consort, always consciously and precisely well dressed, wears a morning coat, medium-deep cravat and a very well fitted pair of checked trousers strapped below the instep. The 16-year old Princess Royal wears a fashionable broad-brimmed hat while the Princesses Alice, Helena and Louise, 14, 11 and nine years respectively, are dressed alike in shaped and basque jackets and knee-length, full skirts with broad-brimmed hats similarly shaped and trimmed. The Prince of Wales, 15 years old, wears a dark jacket and trousers with a smart contrast stripe down the outside seam while his 13-year old brother Alfred wears a double-breasted reefer suit. Arthur, at seven, wears a Highland outfit as popularised by his elder brother in 1846, while Leopold, the youngest of the boys, is four years old and still in petticoats in superficially similar style to those of the girls, though his broad-brimmed hat, as is the mode for boys, accords more with cavalier than country style

137 Hallam Tennison, the five year old son of the Poet Laureate, was photographed by Lewis Carroll (Charles Dodgson) in 1857, wearing a comfortable compromise between dress and tunic, open worked drawers, white stockings and ankle band shoes. The drawers are perhaps regrettably frilly, but in essentials this was normal dress for the average child

Below left

138 The sons of Lord Russell, 1860. They wear knickerbocker suits, the plentiful buttoning on the jacket recalling the modes of the previous generation, though the loose coats with matching waistcoats reflect the easy informality of mid-century masculine fashion. The wide shirt collar is worn outside the jacket and the boys wear wide-brimmed straw hats and slip-on buckle shoes. Striped stockings were as popular with adults as they were for children, but usually less obvious and visible

Opposite

139 The sisters wear matching dresses conventional for 1857, the date of the photograph, with waists at low natural level and reasonably full ankle-length skirts. The sleeves, with ruched trim and flaring cuffs, are fashionable, but the extra under sleeve is more sensible than smart, as is the older girl's schoolroom apron. Their hair, medium-long, is held back in a snood. Stockings are light and the shoes square-toed, fairly heavy and secured with crossed ribbon ties. Their brother wears an Eton suit characterised by its waist length 'bum-freezer' jacket

140 Lady Hawarden photographed three of her daughters in the early 1860s. Her family was so large and closely spaced it is impossible to be certain of the identity and age of the girls shown here. All three, from 'teenager' to the surely 'under tens' wear crinolines, the short skirts of the younger children permitting an extensive view of rather wrinkled, thick-ribbed stockings and side-button boot. The older girl has had problems with one of the fashionable smooth rolled hairstyles

Below

142 Mrs Granville's new baby, photographed with its mother by Silvy in 1865, wears a typical long robe of the period, with low neck, short sleeves and decorative front panel with open work embroidery in the angular design fashionable at the time. Despite some contemporary criticism babies were put into long dresses at birth and were only 'shortened' at about six months of age

Opposite left

143 A formal little boy in a velvet tunic, flared and with a diagonal fastening and a contrast trim, short, plain white drawers, short socks and side-fastening boots. The photograph was probably taken in the mid-1860s and his mother (?) is conventionally fashionable in a dress with a medium-sized crinoline, epaulet and basque trimming

141 'It won't come smooth'. In July 1863, Irene Macdonald, by special request of the photographer Lewis Carroll, posed in her flannel nightdress. It has a rounded collar and long sleeves and is trimmed with narrow frills. Only in its length does it differ from adult nightwear of the period

Right

144 Despite his youth, this small boy has been promoted from dress and drawers to tunic and knickerbockers, set off with horizontally striped socks and side-button boots. Knee-length baggy breeches were called 'knickerbockers' after the seventeenth-century Dutch settlers drawn by Cruikshank in 1859 to illustrate Cholley Knickerbocker's (Washington Irvine's) burlesque *History of the World*. The *carte de visite* dates from the mid-1860s when contrast decoration was very popular and patterns adapted to hand and machine sewing were often to be found in women's magazines of the period

Below right

145 Arthur Myers, photographed about 1862, and probably one of the Highstead students, is young enough to wear a belted tunic, but sufficiently mature for trousers. He carries a flat-crowned, wide-brimmed felt hat

146 The boy pupils at Teston Village School, Kent, 1858–60. Only one, the oldest (or at least the largest), wears a smock, the youngest wear tunics, to which the middle-sized add trousers; only one seems to wear a suit. All have peaked caps

147 A boarding school group, the Highstead Torquay Football Team, 1864–65. The lads wear youthful but fashionable clothes, low-crowned bowlers with loose, hip-length, high-buttoning jackets and wide cut trousers

148 Destitute boys, candidates for the charity of Dr Barnardo, *circa* 1870. They wear haphazardly fitting and tatty but basically conventional boys' clothing, ready made and probably second hand. It is interesting to compare the double-breasted suit worn by the oldest lad with that worn by Prince Alfred in figure 136. The check shirt of the boy in the centre was part of the normal working-class wardrobe. Even though barefoot, for shoes were very expensive, most boys observe the proprieties of the age and wear a hat. There are several soft caps of approximately Glengarry shape and a less battered version of the low-crowned bowler can be seen in figure 147

149 Willie (seated) and Mary (standing) to the
left of the elderly Mrs Nicholson in her
goffered gauze widow's cap, wear dresses
probably made from white cotton, trimmed
with embroidery. By 1866, the date of the
photograph, the embroidery would probably
have been machine rather than hand made.
Names and contemporary inscription apart, it
would be almost impossible to tell Willie from
his sister. The older boy, Herbert, has been
promoted out of 'frocks' and into a kilt with
velvet jacket and waistcoat

Above right
150 Three sisters *circa* 1870, photographed by
J. Rejlander. The girls all wear the same
dresses, with fashionable peplum and contrast
trimming. The length is precisely graduated
according to age – shortest for the youngest.
Their stockings are light and they wear side-
fastening, square-toed boots with 'galoche'
tops and contrast toe caps

Right
151 A boy photographed in 1872 wearing what
outfitters referred to as a 'Single Breasted
(S.B.) Reefer'. It is in scaled down adult style.
In its resemblance to twentieth-century modes
it seems to bely its date, except for the stripe
down the seam of the trousers

152 A small boy of the mid-1870s in a lace and ribbon-trimmed velvet suit, inspired by the 'cavalier' styles of the seventeenth century. It was a mode which was to be popularised by the clothes worn by Little Lord Fauntleroy in the illustrations by Reginald Birch for the book of the same name by Frances Hodgson Burnett, published in 1886, and which despite consistent juvenile resistance remained in children's wardrobes until at least the turn of the century. Straight knee-length trousers began to replace knickerbocker styles during the later 1860s

Above right
153 A very smart little girl in about 1880 wearing one of the new fashioned strict tailor modes, a double-breasted tweed overcoat with a jaunty bowler hat, long, tight, side-button boots and a neatly rolled umbrella with an up-to-date thick twig-like handle

154 The small girls in this photograph of 1882 are wearing shorter versions of the current style for ladies, made from contrasting materials and having the long, fitted bodice with a drape at the hip. Even their hairstyles have the fashionable fringe. The tightness of the adult fashions is, as so often with children's clothes, modified by smocked trimming. Since they are dressed alike, they are probably sisters

155 Kate Rourke and her sister Mary, young actresses *circa* 1880, wear examples of aesthetic reform styling – a Tudorbethan line achieved by smocking and a soft fullness, less restrictive to arm and waist

156 The principles of reform dress affected children's clothes even more than those of grownups. Jersey was appreciated for its warmth and flexibility, and the little girls pictured here in 1883 wear knitted caps and jumpers with short, pleated skirts and deep sashes. They derived from the clothes worn by fishermen and were popular for seaside wear; it is a feminine version of the sailor suit worn by their little brother. He has long trousers – a younger boy might have worn shorts

Opposite
157 For going out, a baby was put into a long, full, warm, caped carrying cloak, usually of fine wool, much trimmed and sometimes with a warm lining. With it was worn a close-fitting bonnet. Styles hardly changed during the second half of the nineteenth century, but the tight frills on the bonnet, the quilted bib and the machine embroidered double flounce of the long robe, all mark the photograph of the Surrey baby as having been taken in the 1880s. Perambulators had been introduced but were not yet generally accepted and most babies were 'aired' in mother's or nurse's arms

158 The more miscellaneous clothes of average girlhood are seen in this school outing in the mid-1880s. The children are obviously dressed in their best and are not unfashionable with their high-trimmed, adult-style hats set square on their heads and with draped, knee-length dresses showing under their hip-length shaped jackets and caped cloaks

159 A spectacular Kate Greenaway inspired mob cap trimmed *en suite* with an openwork edged cape and skirt is worn by the small girl photographed in the later 1880s. She is obviously dressed in her best with a brooch and ribbon rosettes at her neck and on the toes of her ankle-band shoes, bangles over the cuffs of her wrist-length gloves and a wide silk-sash set at fashionable slightly low waist level. Mothers were fond of the picturesque 'regency' styles invented by the popular illustrator Kate Greenaway (1846–1901) and often copied them for their children, in this instance, though, sensibly avoiding the impractical and by now archaic long skirt

160 Pinafores were synonymous with childhood and the small boy wears a useful and decorative well starched pinafore-cum-overdress with a short-sleeved velvet frock. The tartan bows emphasising the shoulder and the fitted natural waist suggest a date in the late 1880s or early 1890s. With it he wears short white open work socks and ankle-band shoes which the skill of this Godmanchester photographer shows as brand new size 4 with an only just indecipherable circular trade mark. On clothes alone it would be impossible to decide whether the sitter was a boy or a girl; the clue lies in the toy whip, a traditional masculine prop in an as yet unaffectedly male chauvinist nineteenth century

161 The blouse and skirt became almost a feminine as well as feminist uniform in the 1890s. The very high, stiff, stud-fastened collar and plain tie secured by a small pearl pin are uncompromising assertions of a claim to sex equality and mark an assault on masculine privilege; but at the same time this young girl hedges her bets by emphasising the feminine charm of a small waist neatly marked by a wide ribbon belt with an elaborate metal buckle and long smoothly brushed hair held back by a large flapper bow. Her awareness of fashionable trends is confirmed by the wide sleeves of her warm tartan blouse and her smoothly fitted skirt

162 A typical middle class family group of the mid-1890s with the frocks of the youngest girls inspired by the dress reform movement and flowing free and unrestricted from gathered yokes. They have soft full sleeves and are altogether very close to the Aesthetic and Rational styles designed by Walter Crane for *Aglaia*, journal of the Healthy and Artistic Dress Union in 1894. The older girl retains the gathered yoke but her dress has been cut closer to adult style with waist at natural level. The oldest of the girls, mature as she seems in her fashionably cut leg-of-mutton sleeved dress, is still of an age to wear her hair down – it was not usually put up until the girl was considered old enough to enter an adult world. The little boy wears a sailor suit, not all that unlike the form introduced in 1846 by the young Prince; his elder brother wears the tight-seamed version of the popular Norfolk suit, known as 'the Brighton', with a deep stiff Eton collar

163 The Sherman twins wear outdoor dress for their photograph in 1895, and look very fashionable with their yoke-collared, full-sleeved coats, magnificently trimmed, wide-brimmed hats and large shaggy muffs. Cloth gaiters were introduced in the 1890s as skirts and boots became shorter, and continued in use well into the next century. The girls, here aged about eight, were American, from a family which bought its wardrobe from the Paris couture

164 'Children paddling at Yarmouth', photographed by Paul Martin in 1892. Despite the breeze all the children wear hats, though how they were anchored – whether by pins or elastic (introduced in the 1860s and now in general use) – it is difficult to see. The smallest girl wears a peaked 'sports cap' such as had been worn by both adults and children of both sexes since the 1880s. As the wind blows up the skirts of the girls' long sleeved summer dresses, one can make out the tucked and frilled petticoats and the similarly trimmed straight knee-length drawers. The smallest children have horizontally striped paddling drawers pinned over their skirts

165 A girl in bathing costume, *circa* 1895. It is an all-in-one striped garment, probably by this time made of cotton or thin serge with contrast trimming at the fashionable square neck and full sleeve. Ladies' costumes were not dissimilar, though the more conservative would have added a skirt

Men's Dress

166 The Ladder from Fox Talbot's *The Pencil of Nature*, 1842–46, was intended to show the record potential of the photograph when a 'group of persons has been artificially arranged and trained by a little practice to maintain an absolute immobility for a few seconds'; It also provides a back view of a gentleman in a light coloured tail coat, at this period worn for formal occasions. It was distinguished by the cut away, square-ended tails, just above knee length, with the central vent flanked by shallow pleats headed by two buttons and was a formalised version of the eighteenth-century coat. The shoulder seam curves up to the high-set rounded collar and the sleeves smoothly set at the shoulder are very long and tight. The similarity to the fashionable feminine outline is very apparent. With it are worn straight cut trousers and lightweight square-toed shoes. The workmen are in waistcoats and shirt sleeves. Their trousers are also straight cut though made wider and of heavier material

167 A study of a sleeping man by Fox Talbot illustrates the voluminous Victorian shirt. It has a high collar supported by the stiff cravat, and wide straight sleeves with the fullness press-pleated into cuffs – here turned back for additional comfort. Jewellery was an important masculine accessory and this watch chain is almost long enough to encircle the neck

168 A magnificent cravat in broad satin and arranged in a four-in hand-knot; the direct ancestor of the modern tie. A portrait of an unknown sitter taken by Fox Talbot in the mid-1840s

Above

169 For his photograph by Hill and Adamson in 1843–45, James Drummond, RSA, the painter, and later Curator of the National Gallery of Scotland, wears an informal suit of 'dittos' – coat, double-breasted waistcoat and trousers, all made from the same light tweed. The coat is single-breasted and loose fitting with flapped pockets set in the low waistline. It is difficult from the view presented to decide whether it is a morning coat or the even more informal 'surtout', since they differ in length only, and both were characterised by rounded front corners. The sleeves are fashionably long and tight, and the wearer has coped with possible inconvenience by turning back the cuff. The tweed, both of the suit and of the Shepherd's plaid shawl draped under his arm, were products of newly established Scottish industries. James Drummond, then a comparatively young man, wears his hair side parted and rather long, with slight side whiskers

170 Thomas Duncan, RSA, ARA (1807–45), the painter, proclaims his artistic independence of the conventions by wearing an unusual straight-cut frock coat with velvet collar and cuffs and double-flapped pockets for a photograph by Hill and Adamson in the mid-1840s

Below left

171 Two young men photographed by Fox Talbot on the church steps at Reading in the later 1840s, wearing the shorter hip-length flared jacket which was then coming into fashion. One wears a bright pair of check trousers. Both wear top hats which, in the characteristic manner of the 1840s, are tall with slightly concave outline

172 Gentlemen's dress did not change very much between the late 1840s and the early 1850s, the date of this ambrotype. Compare the semi-formal double-breasted frock coat with tight lighter coloured trousers strapped under the foot with those in figure 13. The gentleman also wears a tight double-breasted waistcoat and a spotted cravat. The top hat, though still tall, has become shorter and wider than it had been in the previous decade. The hair, still side parted, is assiduously curled, and the sideboards are longer and thicker, and well on the way to becoming side whiskers

173 Isambard Kingdom Brunel, designer and engineer, was photographed in November 1857 by Robert Howlett at the launching of the Great Eastern steamship. He wears a 'morning suit', conventional costume for the professional man distinguished by its waist seam and the rounded front corners of the skirt. The trousers are v. 'l cut despite their mud stains. The buttons at the ankle suggest they are pantaloons, unfashionable, at least according to contemporary fashion plates, but making it possible to adjust a slightly tapering style so as to fit neatly over boots. The hollow-sided, high top hat and the high collar with large loose bow-tied cravat were fashionable in the later 1850s

174 During the late 1850s and early 1860s,
men's clothes became much looser cut and
assumed a characteristically high button line.
This informal tweed suit, single-breasted, and
with its small turn-down collar may have been
what contemporaries would have called a
'Tweedside'. The pattern woven stripe in the
trousers was another popular feature of the
time. The curly hair and bushy side whiskers
are as fashionable as the suit

175 and 176 The quasi military type, 'the
heavy swell', was a notorious figure of fun in
the late 1850s and early 1860s. Caricatured by
E. A. Sothern as Lord Dundreary in the
comedy *Our American Cousin* in 1861, with
whiskers just that little bit longer, jackets
shorter, peg top trousers marginally baggier
and hats even smaller, he became something of
a trendsetter. This view shows 'Lord
Dundreary' in informal velvet lounge jacket
and wide 'window-pane' check trousers. The
distinction is a subtle one, for figure 176 is a
portrait from life of Lieut Tryon of the 48th
Regiment

178 A Norfolk blouse, the predecessor of the
Norfolk jacket, was characterised by pleats,
which gave ease of movement, a belt and
generous pockets. They were popular for field
sports. The 5th Lord Spencer, in this informal
photograph taken about 1860, wears it with
matching trousers and a low crowned bowler
hat, but in the field, knickerbockers and
deerstalkers were the more usual accessories.
Lord Spencer, later Viceroy of Ireland, was
well known for his charm and good looks

177 Diminutive vocalist Frederick Robson was
photographed in an Inverness cape, which was
popular for travelling (always a chilly
business), and introduced in 1859. It was
usually made of heavy tweed and was
distinguished by its hip-length cape and the
cut of its sleeves, semi-attached at the armhole
so that wearing them was optional

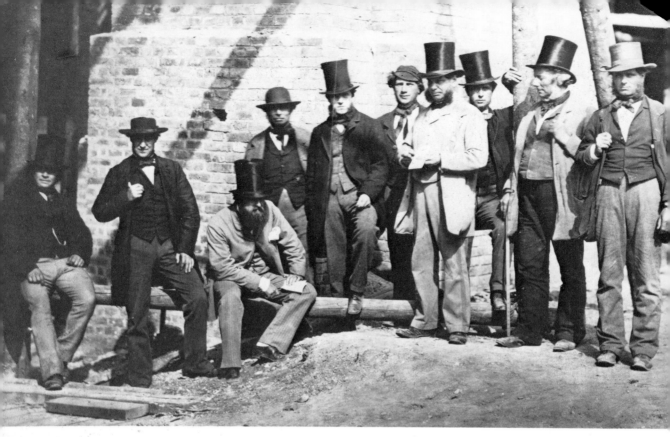

179 Men at work in 1861 – a group of foremen photographed by Cundall and Downes during the preparations for the International Exhibition. Most are wearing miscellaneous and assorted loose hip-length lounge jackets, and the only one with a suit of 'dittos' is their senior member, seated side front. All have sidewhiskers and beards and most wear top hats; the older men seem to have those in a mode with straight sides, the younger ones wearing the more graceful incurving style already seen. The man standing at the back has a peaked cap – the most usual head covering for the working man

180 Albert Edward, Prince of Wales, was conscious of his role as fashion leader even as a very young man, as can be seen from one of his engagement portraits in 1862. He wears a formal frock coat, sleek cut and slightly low-waisted and braid-bound, as is his matching single-breasted waistcoat. New are the slightly lower waistline, the rather deep sleeves, the low turn-down collar and the wide, but not exaggeratedly so, small check trousers in Shepherd's plaid, a Scottish woollen fabric which he is said to have done much to popularise

181 Somewhat flash formal wear is illustrated in this portrait of E. Atkins as the dashing Jim Dalton in *The Ticket-of-Leave Man*, 1863. He wears a loose, light frock coat with check waistcoat and matching baggy peg top trousers. His top hat, set at a jaunty angle, is the tall, almost straight-sided model of the early 1860s

182 A provincial tailor sometimes had problems interpreting fashions in a decade of comparatively rapid change like the 1860s, and the assiduous and detailed guidance of the many men's tailoring guides must on occasion have been confusing rather than enlightening. This photograph, taken in Warrington probably in the early 1860s, shows a gentleman in the exaggeratedly long 'Dundrearies' popularised by E. A. Sothern (see figure 175), with a high-button, high-waisted frock coat and suit of 'dittos' (in what seems from the highlights to have been a very good quality face cloth). The tailor's problem lies in the cut of the front – obviously it is an inexperienced attempt at this high button line. Again, the collar is low and the tie narrow – high collars did not blend easily with whiskers

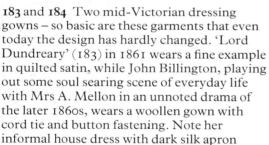

183 and **184** Two mid-Victorian dressing gowns – so basic are these garments that even today the design has hardly changed. 'Lord Dundreary' (183) in 1861 wears a fine example in quilted satin, while John Billington, playing out some soul searing scene of everyday life with Mrs A. Mellon in an unnoted drama of the later 1860s, wears a woollen gown with cord tie and button fastening. Note her informal house dress with dark silk apron

185 This 1864 portrait of A. Lawson and E. Fox Cumberland shows how the style of the date could be comfortably adapted on what, to judge from their luggage, must have been a sketching expedition. They wear loose-fitting, high-button jackets, baggy trousers rolled up to show stout walking boots and small battered felt hats

186 Warrington gentlemen of the mid-1860s in outdoor dress. They wear conventional and well worn overcoats – 'short Chesterfields', with velvet-faced collars and additional ticket pockets. One wears a low-crowned curly bowler hat, the other a medium-low square 'Muller cut down' named after the murderer Muller, who was arrested while wearing one. They wear gloves and carry walking canes, that of the shorter man with an elaborately carved female figure on the handle. The boots, side-fastening, have notably square toes

187 Gentlemen, as this group at Althorp in 1864 illustrates, played cricket in rather miscellaneous summer informal dress. The clothes would have been equally suitable for croquet or boating, the pursuit for which the blazer and boater were originally devised. Noticeable are the horizontally striped cardigan and the short-sleeved jumper (on the reclining figure) and the blazer which, like the hat band and newly invented elastic belts, were probably in the club colours. Headgear is varied and includes boater, bowler and several broad-brimmed felt or straw hats

188 The most popular informal suit from the late 1860s to the end of the century was the double-breasted reefer. It is worn here by the actor E. A. Sothern. With it he wears a soft felt 'Billy-cock' hat. He is an elegant, almost twentieth-century figure, with only the narrow stiff stand collar and string tie to mark more than a century of fashion change

189 'Theodore Baffaire and a lady', photographed by Elliott and Fry in 1872, wear smart morning dress. He has a tweed morning coat and matching waistcoat, the waist higher and the lapel deeper than in the previous decade, and striped trousers, now straight cut. The anonymous 'lady' belies her graceful subservient role by wearing a plain double-breasted almost man-tailored walking jacket over her flounce-trimmed bustle-supported skirt. When jackets of this kind were introduced in the late 1860s, they were considered 'fast' rather than respectable

190 A morning coat characteristic of the mid-1870s, with its deep lapel and markedly diagonal line, from single-button fastening to the sleek cut away double-breasted front. The young man, or his tailor were following closely a *Tailor and Cutter* design of 1876. They have added an extra ticket pocket and made it in a very good quality fabric, the smooth pile of the face cloth gleaming across a century. The trousers, cut to curve gracefully from knee to ankle, are another tribute to the tailor's skill. But what has happened to the sleeve, which is far too long and droopy either for style or for the wearer? The line has more vertical emphasis than in the previous decade, the collar is higher and the cravat is striped and intricately cross-knotted

191 By the late 1870s and early 1880s, the 'University Coat', distinguished by its high sharp cutaway and the opportunity to indulge in fancy pockets and facings, provided the younger man with a smart alternative to the conventionally staid morning coat. This is a notably well made version, for they were said to be difficult to cut correctly. The wearer provides the final touch to his fashionable appearance with a very high 'masher' collar and a carefully barbered hairstyle, swept back precisely from both sides of his centre parting

192 The Prince Imperial, son of Napoleon III, in 1878 dressed in the height of formal fashion in a well tailored, double-breasted frock coat with fashionable low waistline and slightly flared trousers. His collar is high and straight and he wears a neatly folded Ascot cravat with a horseshoe pin. His shoes are much less broad at the toes than they would have been in the previous decade

193 Albert Victor, Duke of Clarence, eldest son of Albert Prince of Wales, was nicknamed 'collars and cuffs' because of the importance he attached to smart dressing. He is the quintessence of 1880s elegance in his single-breasted morning coat and striped trousers cut to break elegantly over the instep of his shoe, and the white 'slip' which sets off the snug fit of his waistcoat. The fashionable line is conspicuously narrow and the coat is high shouldered and high waisted, the vertical emphasis confirmed by the high wing collar and Ascot cravat

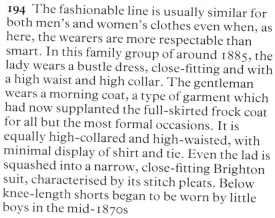

194 The fashionable line is usually similar for both men's and women's clothes even when, as here, the wearers are more respectable than smart. In this family group of around 1885, the lady wears a bustle dress, close-fitting and with a high waist and high collar. The gentleman wears a morning coat, a type of garment which had now supplanted the full-skirted frock coat for all but the most formal occasions. It is equally high-collared and high-waisted, with minimal display of shirt and tie. Even the lad is squashed into a narrow, close-fitting Brighton suit, characterised by its stitch pleats. Below knee-length shorts began to be worn by little boys in the mid-1870s

Above right
195 A single-breasted tweed lounge suit of about 1885. The fashionable narrow, square shouldered line is confirmed by the height of the high-crowned bowler hat. The trousers are straight and rather narrow

196 William Terris, the actor, in the three-button lounge jacket and check 'Tattershall' vest and tweed hat which he wore in *The Bells of Hazlemere* in 1887. The outfit was engraved for the *Tailor and Cutter* for the August of that year

197 The top hat was essential for formal town occasions. It changed shape slowly and by the 1880s was medium-tall with a tapering curve from crown to curly brim, the height of the hat minimised by the deep band. H. B. Conway, the actor, wears it with a frock coat

198 Attempts to reform men's dress were not lacking. Oscar Wilde, who with his wife Constance was a member of the Dress Reform Movement, preferred a satin-faced coat and knee breeches in a Romantic and more or less seventeenth-century style to the unaesthetic 'tubular' garments of his own time. In this photograph by Sarony he is shown in the outfit in which he delighted to shock the audience during his American lecture tour of 1882, to publicise the Gilbert & Sullivan opera *Patience* which satirised the Aesthetic movement

199 Bernard Shaw disapproved of contemporary fashions as class divisive and unhealthy. He found an alternative in a Jaeger suit of wollen jersey, much publicised for its ability to absorb harmful exhalations from the body and, by its particular cut, to provide additional protection for areas considerd exceptionally sensitive to chills, and which he wears in this photograph dated 1885. Bernard Shaw, though not the first, was one of the most effective publicists of the sanitary woollen wares of Dr Gustav Jaeger. Frank Harris reports that Shaw's suit was silver grey in colour and made peculiar scraping noise in movement

200 In the late 1880s, a new garment entered the smart man's wardrobe, the 'dress lounge', what we would call a 'dinner suit'. It was an American innovation and was at first only considered for semi-formal, men-only occasions or dinners at home. G. Haydn Coffin, the musical comedy actor, wears an unusual example with braid fastening in *The Gaiety Girl*, first produced in 1894. He wears it with a formal, low-cut white waistcoat, stiff-bosomed shirt with single pearl stud, narrow white tie and a very high, straight collar. He carries a folding opera hat, a convenient device introduced in the 1840s

201 For at home occasions, smoking jackets provided some respite from the stiff formality of the tailor's suit. E. Willard enacts the 'Spider', the dandy burglar of *The Silver King* in 1888, in a typical example in polka-dotted quilted satin with contrast corded facings

202 These young men, photographed probably on a Blackpool holiday in the 1890s, are wearing single-breasted sports suits typical of the decade with their high-cut lapels and loose square cut. Confirming their informality, the two seated men have the bottoms of their trousers rolled – a sartorial sin in a more formal context, but they still wear high straight stiff collars. The young man at the back wears a contrast jacket and trousers with a cummerbund – an accessory which came into fashion in the middle of the decade. Shoes have changed shape and the toes are now noticeably pointed, even in the soft sports boots worn by the man on the right

203 'Snipe Shooting', a plate from Emerson's *Life and Landscape on the Norfolk Broads*, 1887, shows that shooting dress crossed the classes. Despite the location none wear the conventional 'Norfolk' jacket, but the man at the front wears a shooting coat with flapped pockets and a tweed hat. His neighbour wears waders and a deerstalker hat with ear flaps, the man on the edge of the picture a trilby hat

204 By the end of the century, knickerbocker suits made a convenient and comfortable dress for outdoor pursuits, as shown in this 1894 portrait of the African explorer F. C. Selous. Note the gaiters, the thick-ribbed stockings and stout front-fastening walking boots. The broad-brimmed hat, not included in the country gentleman's usual outfit but which formed part of the equipment of Selous's African expeditionary force, is perpetuated in the uniform of the Boy Scouts, whom their exploits were said to have inspired

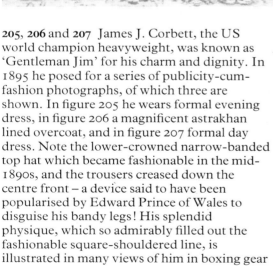

205, **206** and **207** James J. Corbett, the US world champion heavyweight, was known as 'Gentleman Jim' for his charm and dignity. In 1895 he posed for a series of publicity-cum-fashion photographs, of which three are shown. In figure 205 he wears formal evening dress, in figure 206 a magnificent astrakhan lined overcoat, and in figure 207 formal day dress. Note the lower-crowned narrow-banded top hat which became fashionable in the mid-1890s, and the trousers creased down the centre front – a device said to have been popularised by Edward Prince of Wales to disguise his bandy legs! His splendid physique, which so admirably filled out the fashionable square-shouldered line, is illustrated in many views of him in boxing gear

208 In the last decade of the nineteenth century, men's clothes assumed a new fashionable silhouette. It retained its high, square shoulder, but was more broadly and loosely cut, with a slightly lower waist. Austen Chamberlain, photographed by Sir Benjamin Stone outside the Houses of Parliament in 1897, was well known for his incisive elegance. In this photograph he wears a light frock coat with silk facings, light waistcoat and cravat in the 'Joinville' style – that is, fastened by being passed through a clasp or ring. He also carries one of the new lower-crowned top hats

210 Winter clothes as worn by Mr N. Derry, Mr Neville Clarke, Mr J. B. Clarke and Mr Briscoe, photographed by Sir Benjamin Stone outside Studley Castle, Warwickshire, on a snowy January day in 1899. The overcoats are noticeably long, narrow and square-shouldered, though the more sporty Mr Briscoe wears a short fly-fronted covert coat and tweed cap with check knickerbockers and buckle fastening gaiters

209 John Burns, the trade union leader, wore a well tailored lounge suit and bowler hat for his photograph outside Parliament by Sir Benjamin Stone in 1897. Informal clothes were the mark of the labour politician though John Burns's bowler hat was thought to indicate less radical tendencies than Keir Hardie's cloth cap

Occupational and Regional Dress

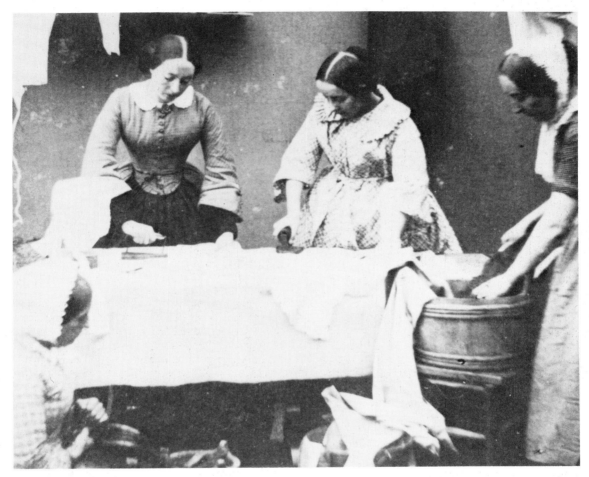

211 'Washing day' – a posed but moderately realistic group from a stereoscopic slide of the mid-1850s. The women wear print dresses with all round gathered skirts of only moderate fullness which can be compared with that worn by Hannah in figure 212. The older women wear caps of reasonably fashionable line and sacking aprons, the youngest woman no cap and a dark almost 'dress' apron: perhaps she is the mistress of the house. The woman to her right wears a print morning wrapper. Hair is drawn back smoothly over the ears, conventionally fashionable but probably much tidier than it would have been in life because washing days were notoriously uncomfortable and exhausting occasions. The older woman is scrubbing linen on a washing board, the youngest ironing and the flat irons and the brazier on which they could be heated can both be seen. Laundry work was a very popular subject for stereo views, the underwear and in some of the later examples, the loose light clothing of the workers, making them temptingly naughty to viewers of the time

212 Hannah, A. J. Munby's beloved, photographed about 1860 in the conventional dress of the middle class maid of all work – a loose-fitting, front-fastening print dress, probably lilac, prettified with a small embroidered collar and brooch, and a small cap with a goffered frill border. Her long sleeves are rolled up and pinned out of the way. She wears a coarse sacking apron to protect her while 'doing the rough'. According to Munby her underwear consisted of a chemise and a coarse stuff petticoat; there is no mention of drawers, which at this time were not usually worn by the working classes. The band around her wrist was leather and played a part in Munby's and Hannah's private drama

213 'Maid of All Work, Dartford', an ambrotype of 1861, from A. J. Munby's collection, is a notably neat figure in her holiday clothes, comprising a fashionable off the face bonnet and an extremely well fitted pretty patterned dress with button and open work border trimming. Wages were not high and it is possible that this dress is a few years old, because the really fashionable sleeve in 1861 flared from the armseye rather than the elbow. Fashion consciousness was a quality which employers tended to deplore; it implied a girl was thriftless – and had ideas above her station

214 and **215** Nan, in the play *Good for Nothing*, played by vivacious Marie Wilton in 1879, attends to her domestic chores. She wears an overall similar in cut to those worn by children. Her polka dot print dress has a tight bodice and an all-round skirt fullness, which makes it closer to the work clothes of the 1860s than the fashionable figure hugging line of the later 1870s. Note its short length

216 A group photograph of the members of the servants' hall at Easton Lodge, Essex, the home of Daisy, Countess of Warwick, in about 1898. The ten maids wear print dresses, starched caps, collars and aprons, while the superior parlour maids are distinguished by their higher and more frilly caps. All the dresses are of print, easy to wash and front fastening. In their midst stands the butler in dark formal clothes with black bow tie. The footmen wear white tie, and have brass buttons on their livery tail coats, the characteristically archaic cut reminiscent of gentlemen's dress at the beginning of the century. The housekeeper, dignified in dark silk, sits in the centre, with cook in a bibbed apron to her right

217 Of the three employees of the Chelmsford Brewery, Essex, photographed in about 1864, two still wear smocks, in essence useful washable agricultural overalls. The decorative stitching, the smocking, which controlled the fullness, was their most characteristic feature. The garments were sometimes made at home, but the majority were the product of small scale rural industries; hence the embroidered design is not an infallible guide either to geographical location or to the occupation of the wearer. The suit worn by the third man seems to be made of fustian, a hard-wearing, cotton-piled fabric

Above right
218 Fox Talbot photographed the Lacock Abbey gamekeeper in the early 1840s. The man wears a fustian waistcoat and trousers, side fastening gaiters (probably of canvas) and a loose lounge type jacket with a soft wide-brimmed felt hat. The contribution made by the working clothes of the 1840s to the leisure wear of subsequent generations is impossible to underestimate

219 Another of A. J. Munby's favourite workgirls, a milkwoman from Sim's Dairy, Jermyn Street, photographed in 1864. The close goffered edged cap, triangular folded shawl, narrow, high-waisted stuff dress and coloured apron were as much a mark of her profession as her yoke and buckets. Milkwomen had worn archaic and distinctive clothes with country overtones ever since the eighteenth century, diffusing an aura of country freshness over dubious town-bred milk

220 'Bringing Home the May', a composite posed photograph which Henry Peach Robinson exhibited in 1862, was applauded by contemporaries for its realism. The clothes are much closer to those worn in realistic painting than in the fashion plates, and as garments in hard everyday use were hardly likely to survive. The gowns are only moderately full, and the central figure has pinned back her skirt to keep it clean in a way common in most peasant communities and which historically can be traced back to the seventeenth century. The women wear a number of variations on the short loose washing jacket, or 'bed gowns' as they were known in the rural context, and hood-like sun bonnets. The little girls wear pinafores, simple, round-necked, sleeveless overalls. They are basic and economical and similar garments were worn well into the twentieth century

221 Pea Pickers at Brotherton, Yorkshire. A gang of female seasonal agricultural labourers whom Munby noticed and had photographed in July, 1863. Their clothes have enough in common with those of field workers in other parts of Britain to suggest that here are the elements of nineteenth-century peasant dress. The women wear easy fitting print dresses with aprons and neckerchiefs or shawls. The bonnet of conventional shape is worn, not tipped back as fashionable, but forward to shade the eyes, while a kerchief shades the back of the neck. The least depressed figure is the oldest, standing on the left of the group. She has a flower-bordered shawl and a neat frilled cap, and only her dirty apron marks her pursuit. Since she lacks a basket she may be a forewoman. It is instructive to compare these workers actually engaged in 'bringing home the peas' with the acclaimed realism of the popular 'Bringing Home the May' (220)

222 A group of hop pickers taken by Mr Boyer, the Sandwich cameraman, who photographed several groups, mainly from Cottenden, near Shulden, Kent when, in the mid-1880s he began to work outside his studio, using the more portable dry-plate camera. The three seated ladies, possibly workers who came from London, have protected their average fashionable and not over seasonable clothes with light aprons. They still wear town-style hats. The deep-brimmed straw hat and crochet shawl of the lady standing at the centre back suggest she is a village woman. Note the elaborate cap worn by the baby and the hats of the children

223 A drink break in the hop fields in the 1880s. The men are probably local labour and they wear the washable drill jackets and trousers in some areas known as 'sloppies' (from 'slop', the archaic word for ready-to-wear clothes), produced in factories, and by the last quarter of the nineteenth century readily available even in small towns. The beard worn by the man on the left is an unusual feature at this period, and may suggest that he is a coasting seaman from nearby Sandwich – he appears in several groups. He wears the peaked cap and brass buttoned velvet waistcoat worn by workmen – those photographed by Boyer in Kent and from other parts of the country as well. The hats are varied and the fur or plush caps appear in artisan contexts more or less continuously from the seventeenth century onwards

224 A plough team near Sandwich in the 1880s, another of Boyer's agricultural scenes. The men wear heavy trousers of corduroy (the most usual material for country work clothes at this period), which the man in the centre supports with braces kept from slipping by being knitted through the ends of his neckerchief. Rather unusually, they have a square fall front fly: a sensible if old fashioned style, because it was more hardwearing than the straight fly. For ease of movement the ploughman has tied his trousers below the knee. In some counties such ties were called 'liggets'. His wide-brimmed straw hat may not be conventional fashion but it has utility and years of history for its justification

225 P. H. Emerson's Norfolk peasants (plate II, 'Towing the Reed') from *Life and Landscape on the Norfolk Broads*, 1887. The foremost man wears a jean coat over a high-necked waistcoat, with a muffler. His long waterproof boots are a necessity, albeit an expensive one, for marsh dwellers. His male companion wears one of the characteristically Norfolk boat smocks. Both wear distinctively high conical felt hats with dished brown crowns. The woman wears a belted blouse, short skirt and high boots. She wears a wide-brimmed conical straw bonnet, sensibly if unfashionably tilted forward to shade the eyes

Below

227 A typical countrywoman in close ribbon-trimmed bonnet, tightly pinned crochet shawl and dress, which concedes a little to fashionable niceties. This lady was photographed by W. Boyer in his Sandwich studio, but she has her equivalent in almost every local late nineteenth-century photographer's studio throughout the length and breadth of England

226 George Clausen saw and photographed this country woman topping turnips in 1887, during one of his walks with his Marion spy camera, whose lens was fast enough to take a subject completely unaware and unposed. He was seeking pictorial references for his paintings. The woman has an utter naturalism and primitive power which transcends the conventional studio image. It is a cold winter day and she wears a tattered check shawl and a man's coat over a sacking apron and a multitude of tattered petticoats. Her bonnet is so battered by wind and weather its fashion is indecipherable, and she wears man's boots

Right

228 A Sandwich couple photographed by Boyer in his studio in the High St, Sandwich, in the 1880s. The woman wears a country compromise with fashion – a smart hat tilted too far back and a draped tied-back dress with the shoulders huddled under one of the ubiquitous country shawls. The young man (probably her new husband, for it has the look of a wedding photograph), is probably one of

the local seamen as he has a small beard, pattern knit jersey and sleeved and metal-buttoned velvet waistcoat which seems to have been their local garb. He has many similarly dressed companions in the Boyer archives. It seems probable that the umbrella, substantial as it is, should have really been held by the lady

229 Bricklayers, photographed by Fox Talbot at Lacock Abbey in the mid-1840s wear short workmen's jackets, and round caps and skull caps with earflaps, garments worn in workaday context since at least the beginning of the nineteenth century

Below left

230 Navvies at Redland, Bristol, photographed in 1854. Like most peripatetic gang labour they tended to adopt a unique form of dress, and the combination of a light, broad and curly-brimmed hat, a kerchief and a sleeved, double-breasted, buttoned waistcoat, contemporaries would have found distinctive and recognisable, even though, with the exception of the hat there was nothing unique in any individual garment. The older man wears layers of waistcoats and an exceedingly battered, but not particularly old fashioned top hat. His shirt, over voluminous to our eyes, should be compared with that in figure 167. The sleeves were straight-set and a loose cut was necessary for ease of movement

Opposite

231 Female mine tip workers from Tredegar, South Wales; a photograph from a series by W. Clayton, a local photographer for an album compiled by C. B. Crisp – perhaps a Munby-like amateur inspector. The photographs are now in the Gallery of English Costume, Manchester. Like other gang labour, the girls had developed a group image according to the contemporary description which accompanies the photograph and wore 'a peculiar style of dress . . . a short frock and apron, tight to the neck . . . of hop cloth a fine sacking, red worsted stockings and lace up boots, heavy with hobnails, tips and toecaps . . . The bonnet or hat, for it is difficult to discern to which . . . this head dress belongs, is bedecked with beads, brooches and feathers'

232 Henry Neville, the actor, was immediately recognisable in his Welsh miner's dress to all who saw him in 1867, searching for his errant daughter in the melodrama *Lost in London*. A flannel shirt probably blue in colour, 'moleskin' trousers and heavy work clogs all figured in the working wardrobe of the pitman, though neither invariably nor necessarily all at the same time

233 Ellen Grounds, a Wigan collier girl, was photographed in 1873 with and at the wish of that champion of the Victorian female manual labourer, A. J. Munby, here seen in conventional mid-Victorian travelling dress of tweed lounge suit and low crowned 'Muller cut down' hat. He has turned the bottom of his trousers up, perhaps in tribute to the dust of toil. The night before, Munby had checked

through Ellen's clothes – the 'wadded hood bonnet ... "mah bedgoon" of pink cotton patched with bits of blue and "mah breeches" ... men's old breeches which after a year were all patches of cloth and cotton and linen of various colours but toned down by coal dust to a blackish brown. They were warmly lined and wadded especially at the knees to protect them ... how did she keep them on? "there's a mony wenches ties string around their waists but ahve gotten a good backside, as keeps me breeches oop"'. She wears a petticoat of striped cotton 'rolled up as a joiner rolls his apron; it is never let down and is perfectly useless – only retained as a symbol of sex'. The words taken from Munby's diary, are his own. When the weather was cold the girls wore waistcoats or short thick 'peacoats'. Ellen also wears brass-tipped clogs

234 Fisherwomen at Newhaven near Edinburgh photographed by Hill and Adamson in 1845, to assist in a fund-raising campaign for a new boat. The women's clothes have evolved from the dress of the late eighteenth-century female agricultural worker's in a way which was particularly suited to their calling. It comprised a printed cotton 'bedgown', a T shaped jacket with straight-cut sleeves wrapped over and held by the formally draped up apron, under which can be seen the striped petticoat. They wear kerchiefs on their heads, sometimes over their goffer frilled caps. The kerchiefs cross at the chin and tie at the back, so that, together with the hood of the knee-length cape, they form a protective pad for the creel

235 'Fishermen ashore': Alex. Rutherford, William Ramsay and John Liston, from Newhaven near Edinburgh, photographed by Hill and Adamson in 1845. They wear waist-length jackets and wide straight canvas trousers with fall fronts. In other pictures the trousers can be seen tucked into heavy sea boots. They have neckerchiefs and hats in variety. Clothes of this kind are worn by many seafaring men of the time

236 The cockle and bait collectors at Filey were another delight for ankle starved Victorian voyeurs, as this view of them taken in 1865–67 by Walter Fisher, a local photographer, suggests. The girls wear clothing similar to that of other fisher women, namely cotton frocks, hood bonnets and shawls, but the physical features of the bay, necessitating scrambling up Flamborough Head on a rope, led to them tucking up their short blue skirt or 'fishing kirtle', pinning it around their knees, or even wearing knee breeches. It is another print from A. J. Munby's 'working women' collection

237 Holiday visitors found the distinctive local and occupational dress of the fisherwomen of Tenby characteristic enough for Francis Frith to record it in a photograph in 1890. In essence it is similar to that of other countrywomen in having a tightly pinned shawl and full skirt. It was the shortness of the skirt (a necessity for any woman shore worker), the picturesque arrangement of the laced, blue, sleeveless bodice, the kerchief and the broad brimmed black 'wide awake' hat which made them unusually colourful. Their clothes have analogies with the dress of the fisherwomen of the nearby village of Llangwym, which had delighted by A. J. Munby a generation before this picture was taken

238 and **239** The fishing community of
Whitby, Yorkshire, was immortalised by
Frank Sutcliffe in the late nineteenth and early
twentieth century. These photographs are
taken from the series of 'snapshots' that he took
for Kodak, not from the better known posed
views. They are unusual in that they show the
fishermen and women in their actual working
clothes, not as so often, cleaned up for the
camera. In figure 238 taken about 1890, the
men offloading on the jetty wear boat smocks
and jumpers protected by waterproof aprons,
seaboots and caps, both the hard-topped
'engine cap' and the conventional sporty
variety, perhaps even better adapted for box
carrying. For onshore wear, the men wear
jumpers and normal lounge jackets and
trousers with the high-crowned bowler of the
period. The women in figure 239, from the cut
of their blouse sleeves, may have been
photographed around 1905 and have working
aprons over their skirts. The three younger
women wear respectively the traditional
kerchief, a semi-fashionable hat and a sports
cap, again very adaptable as working head gear.
The older woman still has the sunbonnet with
its distinctive turned back brim and narrow
fluted curtain so often to be seen in Sutcliffe's
earlier posed views. She also wears a check
apron over her dark, probably black bodice and
skirt. The picture is interesting in that it shows
how new work clothes are supplanting the old,
relegated now to semi-practical regional dress.
The cable pattern of the old man's jumper is
typical of the design used for the warm
waterproof garments, the knitting of which is
now recognised as a local speciality of fishing
communities

240 In Liverpool, the town of the great mid-century Irish immigration, and in Manchester, it was quite usual to see women wearing shawls draped over head and shoulders in the style reminiscent of the traditional Irish mantle. In the cotton towns of the north west they had the additional advantage of protecting the wearer from the chill of the outside after the hot, steamy atmosphere of the cotton factory. With the shawl, these women, 'Shawlies' in Manchester and 'Mary Ellens' in Liverpool, wore the dress of poor women anywhere, short skirts and miscellaneous blouses or bodices. Many wore clogs, traditional in Lancashire and Yorkshire, though not to be seen in this view of the Flat Iron market, Chapel Street, Salford, by S. L. Couthurst, 1894

241 An old clothes shop in Seven Dials, photographed by J. Thomson for *Street Life in London* in 1877. Hanging up are the clothes most in demand on the second-hand market, namely washing skirts and dresses; not that the proprietor or the customer are in the least affected by changes of fashion, for in hair and garb they are far more characteristic of the 1860s than the 1870s

242 The shellfish stall, from J. Thomson's
Street Life in London, 1877. The stallkeeper
wears a random accumulation of overskirt,
underskirt and bodice – none of which match –
together with a sacking apron. The man on the
right wears a high-crowned felt hat, an unusual
collared waistcoat with double curved pockets,
and notably well-cut, tapering trousers with
lapped seams. He may possibly be a coster,
who both before and after the classic account of
their life and characteristics given by H.
Mayhew in his *Life and Labour of the London
Poor*, 1851–62, were distinguished by special
and not inexpensive clothes. The shabby but
formally dressed man by his side wears a high-
crowned bowler and a short morning coat,
characteristic of the late 1870s and 1880s

Opposite

243 and **244** Coster lads and their girlfriends
enjoying themselves on a Bank Holiday at
Hampstead Heath in 1895, unobtrusively
recorded by Paul Martin. The coster girls'
dresses approximate to the fashionable, though
the hip-length bodices and wide-brimmed hats
trimmed with great toppling piles of flowers
and feathers mark their caste and class. The
bystanders, much more plainly dressed, wear
plain wide-brimmed boaters similar to those in
figure 123

245 The archetypal schoolmaster of Victorian England, the scholar cleric, professionally qualified to cope with both the minds and the morals of his charges; the former marked by his university cap and gown, the latter by his 'dog collar' and clerical suit. This photograph shows the Headmaster of Rugby

246 Samuel Wilberforce (1807–73) successively Bishop of Oxford and Winchester, in his regulation episcopal outdoor dress in the 1870s. He wears an apron, short surplice, a frock coat, presumably knee breeches, and gaiters, and carries a low-crowned, curly-brimmed top hat

Opposite
247 William Boyd Carpenter, Bishop of Ripon, in his vestments, rochet and chimere. Taken by Barraud in the 1870s

248 Sir Benjamin Stone photographed the
Vicar and local deputation at the Leicestershire
Hallaton Pie Festival for his *Pictures circa*
1900. The Vicar is conventional clerical in
broad-brimmed hat, dog collar and suit –
consciously archaic in its cut, being basically a
frock coat with an eighteenth-century type
standing band collar. His parishioners wear
their tweed suits – jackets made with trousers,
knickerbockers or riding breeches and gaiters –
whichever seemed most convenient for a very
quaint local custom of a fight with lumps of
hare pie, followed by a football game with a
small firkin of beer. It was an ancient Easter
pastime such as could be only justified by
charity and sanctified by tradition

249 The newly elected Alderman Waterlow,
for the commemorative portrait taken by his
son in 1863, wears a fairly characteristic
English ceremonial accumulation of historical
costume. His velvet and fur-faced Alderman's
gown is based on sixteenth-century models,
while his court suit, with its cut steel buttons
and embroidered waistcoat is derived from late
eighteenth-century styles

250 A group of civic dignitaries: the Sheriff in
his trained and tufted legal mantle, flanked by
the Mayor and Alderman in their chains and
furred gowns, and mace bearer in his cloak and
three-cornered hat. They were photographed
outside Lichfield Guildhall by Sir Benjamin
Stone as part of his record of the Lichfield
Greenhill Bower, which is described in his
Pictures as a democratic 'court of Arraye and
View of Arms' and having its origins in the
eleventh century. The ceremonial dress of the
local dignitaries, with their prototypes in the
sixteenth century for the county and municipal
dignitaries, and the eighteenth for the mace
bearer, links nineteenth-century England with
its past and traditions

251 By 1894, the date of this Welsh Tea Party, by Francis Frith (the basis of a series of picture postcards and miscellaneous souvenirs still available in any Welsh resort), Welsh national dress had become summarised and vulgarised into a black chimney pot hat, said to have sixteenth-century origins, and worn over a goffered cap common to most countrywomen, together with an all-enveloping red caped cloak, conventional in most of rural Britain from the eighteenth century onwards. Under was worn a full-skirted dress, usually of Welsh flannel, and an apron. Welsh national dress had been developed by Lady Llanover, a somewhat eccentric nationalist, based on the clothes worn by Welsh country women in the early nineteenth century

252 John Francis Campbell of Islay
photographed by Hill and Adamson *circa* 1845
wears a Glengarry bonnet, plaid kilt and
sporran, with a conventional shirt jacket and
waistcoat. It is Scottish dress as actually worn
in the Highlands, not the coarsened and
popularised version based on military
prototypes sometimes even hired out by
Scottish photographers to those who wished to
parade their nationalism – or merely ape the
aspirations of the Royal Family at Balmoral

253 The old men from Skye, *circa* 1890, show their national allegiance only in their tuft-topped soft Glengarry bonnets. Otherwise their clothes are unexceptional for their age and generation – tweed suit and a velvet or fustian coat and waistcoat

Appendix

QUOTATIONS FROM CONTEMPORARY SOURCES

Ladies' dress in the 1840s

During the 1840s, in times of trade depression, long cold winters and hot though short summers, the pace of fashion moved slowly:

The time is past when great and sudden changes took place in fashion. We never go now from one extreme to the other.

The Ladies' Cabinet, 1844

We have been obliged of late to repeat that the forms of robes, whether for morning or evening dress have suffered very little change, as regards the *corsage*; this is not only literally true, but it is very right . . . for we never remember fashion and reason so completely in unison, since whether the *corsage* is high or moderately low, it cannot be made in a manner more becoming to the shape.

The Ladies' Cabinet, 1847

The style with which they seem so bored, and about which they are so complacent, has a long tightly fitted bodice low cut for evening and generally high cut for day with a deeply pointed waistline to which a softly full floor-length skirt is tightly gathered. Sleeves are tight, long for day and short for evening. It is a line established by the end of the previous decade:

I hope you who are so fashionable a person have already made all your sleeves quite tight to your arm . . . I know you will not think of going out with such an old fashioned thing as a full sleeve at present.
Cecilia Ridley, *Life and Letters of Cecilia Ridley, 1819–45*, letter of May 1837

Pointed corsages are decidely the mode . . . indeed no others are worn.

World of Fashion, 1838

Full sleeves and short round waists still linger among the elderly and unfashionable in the early 1840s, though for the up-to-date skirts are set in tight low gathers:

By gauging all round the top as far as the points of the hips, by this means that excessive fullness which would be otherwise disposed of in gathers or plaits is formed exactly to the shape but on the other hand this method lengthens the waist excessively and gives an air of stiffness to the figure.

World of Fashion, 1841

By 1844 there are signs of change and for morning (informal) dress:

pointed corsages are now entirely abandoned . . . but a good many robes have the corsages rounded gradually on the entire front.

The Ladies' Cabinet, 1844

As the waist slowly begins to rise again, the skirts

. . . increased in width and flounces for which there is a decided vogue add to their enormous voluminosity. Trimmings disposed on the front of the skirt also keep their vogue.

Ibid.

Sleeves shorten:

Demi long sleeves are much in favour

Ibid.

and vary:

. . . there is a good deal of variety in the sleeve; tight ones are very extensively seen, but in general they have some kind of trimming to take off from the extreme plainness.

Ibid.

Materials are soft and flowing. Stripes are popular and patterns somewhat larger in scale than in the 1830s.

Accessories
Mantles are conventional winter wear, and there are several examples of the popular alternative, the shawl, at this period often a square folded to a triangle. Lightweight ones might be of lace and heavier ones of wool generally with a woven or printed pattern. The Indian cone or pine pattern, generally called 'Paisley' after one of the largest shawl centres, was very popular. Similar garments were to remain in use for the next twenty-five years. In the second half of the decade, short shaped jacket bodices begin to be worn. Scarves were as popular with the fashionable as with the photographer looking for a useful prop:

We must . . . observe that scarfs are still in the ascendant; we see them in various materials, in almost all colours . . .

Ibid.

Lingerie dress trimings, collars and cuffs of lace and white-work accompany almost every dress. They were functional as well as decorative and a deep semi-full-dress decolletage could be filled or covered with a collar for less formal occasions. The elderly still wear the wide collars of the previous decade.

Underwear

Underwear is implied rather than seen except by the all too visible ridge around the top of the torso left by the long stiff corset:

The modern stay extends not only over the bosom but also over the abdomen and back down to the hips, besides being garnished with whalebone to say nothing of an immense wooden, metal or whalebone busk, passing in front from the top of the stays to the bottom ... the gait of the English women is generally stiff and awkward, there being no bend nor elasticity of the body on account of the form of her stays.

The Handbook of the Toilet, 1841

The full gathered and rather heavy skirt required support which was provided by at least two and often more petticoats starched and/or reinforced for stiffness. A tournure or bustle at the back provides additional fullness. In the fashion plates the skirts increase in size during the decade but in the photographs the same gentle fullness seems to prevail throughout.

Contemporary standards of decorum and the length of the skirt preclude any view of the square-toed shoes or generally white stockings.

Coiffure

The hair is smoothly dressed and parted in the centre with the side fronts in ringlets or bands so arranged as to leave the ear uncovered and the back hair is knotted on the crown.

The mature wear caps, light wired gauzy structures trimmed with ribbons or flowers, over which the bonnet is sometimes placed. These are large and worn straight on the head, with the brim projecting to conceal the face in profile:

It is now a settled thing that the horizontal line will retain its vogue,

The Ladies' Cabinet, 1845

The 1850s and early 1860s

The 1850s and early 1860s were a time of economic optimism and expansion, characteristics reflected in the clothes of the ladies. The period was ushered in by the Great Exhibition of 1851, the first of the series of international exhibitions which were to stimulate and commemorate expansion of trade and industry in the second half of the nineteenth century.

One of the most significant inventions in this context was the sewing machine, invented early in the century but not in general use until the later 1850s and 1860s. 'Mechanised' sewing was quicker and

clothes became cheaper and more plentiful. Styles spread rapidly from class to class and from place to place but still, especially in this period of Free Trade, Paris fashions dominate. The smart world finds a new ideal of elegance in the Empress Eugénie, married to Napoleon III in 1853, and then in the tall fair Alexandra, Princess of Wales married in 1863. The French couture which in the popular mind was synonymous with Charles Frederick Worth (1824–95) becomes the arbiter of taste in dress.

Initially, dresses retain the line of the late 1840s, with tight bodices and full skirts gathered into a medium-low waist.

Evening dresses retain the low pointed waist, but for day the waistline straightens and rises until by the end of the period it is rather above than below the natural level. It is difficult to plot this with exactness because most fashion comment concentrates on the increasing spread of the skirt, the breadth of which, especially when worn with higher heels, makes the waist look higher.

I regret to say the waist exhibits a tendency to emulate those of our great-grandmamas – a fashion so graceless and unnatural, that it can only be regarded as a temporary caprice.

New Monthly Belle Assemblée, 1860

The waist is emphasised:

Ribbon or velvet *waistbands*, brocaded or embroidered are amongst the novelties of the season.

Englishwoman's Domestic Magazine, 1861

The skirt becomes steadily more full, its breadth emphasised by trimming:

Parisian authorities are determined that ladies ... must purchase new [dresses], for revolutions have taken place. The plain skirt of very rich material has usurped the place of the *robe à quilles* or *à la militaire* ... This fashion from the ease with which it could be adopted, was exposed at its first appearance to the danger of soon becoming very common. But although the plain skirt is adopted, many skirts are still to be seen profusely trimmed, but seldom or never down the side. The trimmings are placed round the skirt, and they are of the same colour as the dress. Even one flounce has found favour in some eyes; and rich trimmings down the front of the skirt are in vogue ... for general wear the Bodices of dresses are made either pointed before and behind, or round ... Double skirts are still seen, as also flounced skirts. The upper skirt should be ornamented with three narrow flounces.

The Ladies' Treasury, 1858

Dresses such as these used a great deal of material, and:

Many persons have their dresses made now with two bodices, so that they may be used for evening toilets or those moins habillés ...

Englishwoman's Domestic Magazine, 1861

Skirts are balanced by a similar development in the sleeve, which becomes shorter and wider until by the end of the decade the fullness can spring directly from the armhole.

There is at present no change in the shape of sleeves; ... they are ... of a three-quarter length, and of the funnel shape; except those that are open at the wrist to the elbow; and those that are nearly the same width from bottom to top.

New Monthly Belle Assemblée, 1851

Sleeves are made flat at the top of the arm and open from the bottom to the elbow, showing the full tulle or muslin undersleeve, or the thicker muslin one in a morning dress.

The Ladies' Treasury, 1858

In the early 1860s, new sleeve forms are introduced, still full, but longer, and tighter at the wrist:

Plain sleeves are also in the ascendant; ... When the sleeve is quite close to the arm, it has generally an epaulet or puffing or flounce at the shoulder ...

New Monthly Belle Assemblée, 1860

We will give two or three *sleeves* suitable for ordinary dresses, 1. A bishop sleeve, with a narrow wristband. 2. A bishop sleeve, the fulness gathered into a band the length of the arm, ... 3. A sleeve perfectly tight to the elbow, and finished off at the top with two puffings and a trimming to correspond with that on the dress.

Englishwoman's Domestic Magazine, 1861

Frills and directionally patterned fabrics made the dresses look larger than they actually were:

ROBES A DISPOSITION are expected to be among the most fashionable of the spring silks. That name is given to them because the grounds are always flowered, and the robes trimmed with flounces; each flounce bordered with a wreath of flowers corresponding with those of the ground.

New Monthly Belle Assemblée, 1851

Light colours for fabrics are replaced by brighter colours, some the product of the new chemical dye industry:

Plain full colours are very much in vogue in silks, woollens and *fabrics de fantasia*, the most popular and serviceable of which we predict will be those that come under the general name of *reps* or corded surfaces ... In silks, longitudinal stripes and *jacquard* figures predominate. *Magenta* blushes everywhere and in every thing, from *jupons* to neckties, and rich shades of plum and claret promise to be popular; for the rest, greens of various tints, *Azof* especially, with *mauves* and browns and blues are the prevailing colours.

New Monthly Belle Assemblée, 1860.

After 1860, plain fabrics are preferred to the patterned and the bulk of the dress, usually impressive enough in its own right, is emphasised by contrast bands and braid patterns often applied with a sewing machine. Geometric effects are preferred to floral motifs. Trimmings are concentrated at the hem.

Underwear

The key to the increased width of the skirt is the introduction of the cage crinoline, a light rounded metal framework, supported by hoops or petticoat. It was introduced in 1855 and mass production methods made it cheap and readily available. Occasionally dangerous and often derided, they

were so comfortable ... kept the petticoat away from your legs and make walking so light and easy.

G. Raverat, *Period Piece*, 1954

The convenience was obvious when

some Belles wear sixteen petticoats for evening dress.

New Monthly Belle Assemblée, 1856

They were not always easy to wear or control and an early critic remarks:

They are easily recognised in the street by 'sagging' – no other word will exactly convey the idea – from side to side of the hoops, an effect which is distinctly visible as the wearer walks along.

Mrs Merrifield, *Dress as a Fine Art*, 1854

The ridge made by the hoop, when incorrectly sized or inadequately covered by the petticoat, is as characteristic of the period as the corset ridge of the previous decade. Corsets were of course still worn, but they were shorter and less stringent.

As the summer advances there is one caution we must offer our subscribers, and that is to remember that these hoops are most ungraceful unless their contour is entirely concealed by an abundant flow of the drapery of the underskirt – when the stiff outlines are visible, we cease to wonder at the severe reflection cast upon the much censured and widely adopted crinoline.

Englishwoman's Domestic Magazine, 1859–60

Crinoline 'a balloon on a ring fence'.

The Warehousemen and Drapers' Trade Journal, 1878
(retrospectively)

With the sway of the hoop and a vogue for shorter skirts for day, petticoats were often visible and tended to be decorative with border patterns. Red was a popular colour and for outdoor informal wear, when skirts were kilted up.

Petticoats are being trimmed almost as much as dresses, and as now every lady in the street shows more of the former than of the latter garment it is absolutely necessary that they be tastefully got up.

C. W. Cunnington, *Englishwoman's Costume in the 19th century*; unstated source in 1863

Footwear

Stockings became more decorative and shoes began to acquire heels, for the first time since the eighteenth century. Even in 1854, Mrs Merrifield in *The Art of Dress* was worried by the introduction of a one inch heel, but by the early 1860s this could be as much as three inches high. Overshadowed by the monstrous structures above, they are not easy to see in photographs. The extent of the grey area below the hemline shows the real skirt length as opposed to the fashion plate ideal or caricature comment.

Outerwear

Shawls continue to be worn:

Cashmere shawls, always so much in favour in spring and autumn, are now extensively seen. Square shawls are generally adopted for the promenade, and long ones in carriage-dress ... the patterns are arabesques and palms, in rich and brilliant colours but they do not afford any novelty. I may say the same of China crape shawls, also expected to be very much in vogue during the early part of the spring.

New Monthly Belle Assemblée, 1851

However, these are rivalled by cloaks and mantles which fall straight and unwaisted from shoulder to hip.

... the summer *burnous*. This article of toilette is intended to be worn on leaving the ball or the opera, and also during the afternoon promenade. ... It should have a hood, and in its depth equal the modern opera cloak.

The Ladies' Treasury, 1858

A new development is the waist-length jacket which when worn with blouse and skirt, combined variety with economy. It was popularised by the young Princess Alexandra in 1862–63 and points the way to a vogue for jackets and skirts.

... winter fashions; but in all probability the mantle will be much worn. Cloth jackets with metal buttons, have made their appearance.

Ibid.

The success of the *Zouave* vests is quite astounding, and both for home wear and the theatre they are certain to be the vogue this year. The former are generally of cloth or *cachemire* garnished with *soutache*; ... The *Zouaves* are made either closed or open, and more or less adjusted to the figure ... In fact this most conquettish vest is made to suit all caprices ...

New Monthly Belle Assemblée, 1860

Coiffure

After a decade in which very little change is seen, hair and headdress styles change rapidly in the 1850s and 1860s.

Caps are still worn indoors but only by the mature:

Young married ladies need not wear caps until they acquire the endearing name of 'Mother'.

C. W. and P. Cunnington *Handbook of English Costume in the 19th century* quoting from an unattributed source, 1857

... little change in the form of *chapeaux*. The brims are expected to continue quite round, or ascending to the oval, small, and almost meeting under the chin; the crowns will continue low, and the *bavolets* moderately deep and full, standing out from the throat. I need hardly observe that the shape of the brim renders a good deal of trimming in the interior necessary.

New Monthly Belle Assemblée, 1851

and then become smaller and by 1853 begin to change in style and angle:

It is the peculiar form of the crown which gives this appearance, by being made low and sloping towards the back.

World of Fashion, 1853

In the second half of the decade, they are triangular in profile and leave the whole front of the head bare. The centre front of the brim develops and becomes higher and projects forward so that the bonnet assumes an oval 'spoon' shape in profile.

The front is slightly pointed, rather deeper than formerly, more open at the sides of the face ...

Englishwoman's Domestic Magazine, 1858

Hats, rather than bonnets, begin to be worn for less formal occasions and are especially popular with the young. They appear first in the late 1840s but become generally fashionable only in 1854–55.

The ladies are at present wearing a broad flapping slouched hat of brown chip which overshadows their features like a huge parasol. It is only occasionally seen in the town but is very common in the country and particularly at the seaside.

The Illustrated London News, 1855

It was followed by other shapes which remained broad-brimmed in the late 1850s, while smaller and more masculine shapes began to predominate in the early 1860s.

The basic shape of the 1840 hairstyling is retained, with its centre parting and knot at the back of the head, but there was considerable change in the arrangement of the side hair and placing of the 'bun' during this decade. It is indeed a most sensitive indication of date.

In 1850–51, a loosening of the style is apparent; the side hair is puffed over the ear, half concealing it, and the knot at the back slips below the crown of the head.

The popularity of Eugènie, new Empress of France in 1853, introduced a new way of dressing the hair, copied from the one she habitually wore. Its critics dubbed it 'barefaced' and it was distinguished by having the hair slightly puffed at crown and sides, but rolled away from the face, thus emphasising the forehead and leaving the ears visible. There were sometimes 'Kiss curls' on the cheeks. It remained popular in modified form until the end of the decade, though it by no means appealed to all or suited all faces. Some considered it

bold, masculine and in most cases very disfiguring.

The Ladies' Treasury, 1858

An alternate and somewhat softer style, introduced in 1856, and very popular in the late 1850s and early 1860s, was the Coiffure Ristori in which the crown is left smooth and the sides turned under in a smooth roll which is tucked into a bun worn more or less at the nape of the neck. A popular compromise was to have a series of curls at the side, parallel with the parting. The chignon, always worn low in the late 1850s and early 1860s, tends to become bigger, and curls pendant from it were worn by the young for day as well as evening.

The change within a decade is dramatic; demure modesty has become ostentation:

For a series of years the simplicity of the *coiffure* enabled ladies with their maid's assistance, almost to dispense with hairdressers, and to arrange their own tresses. What more simple than the bands in front and the hair plaited behind. But strange to say when fashion, in adopting the *coiffure* 'à l'impératrice', intimated that the face needed neither shade nor softening influence, it also decided that the head could not be too richly *adorned* not to say *loaded* with hair ... In all the *coiffures*, whether 'à l'impératrice', 'à la Fontanges', or 'à la Victoria' ... To dress the front hair you must, in the first instance, part it down the middle, comb it back over a *frisette* or *rouleau*, and carrying the ends of the hair to the back of the head, conceal them under a plait.

Ibid.

With bonnets growing so small ... hair getting cleaner and cleaner; until the eye is now continually delighted with the sight ... curls no longer resembling (to use Thackeray's remark) 'damp black snakes' better than the masses of greasy heavy looking hair with which our eye and nose have been assailed.

Englishwoman's Domestic Magazine, 1858

... for evening ... for the hair, round wreaths are decidely in favour. Those formed of grass have been patronised by the empress, and are consequently fashionable. Long *barbes* falling on the shoulders surmounted by roses of different shades form a stylish headdress. Field daisies are also seen woven into wreaths, with poppies and buttercups.

The Ladies' Treasury, 1858

Fashions are extrovert and begin to be ostentatious:

It never occurs to them that bonnets of the 'kiss me quick' build, loud stockings, exaggerated tournures, capes and crinolines; vagrant ringlets straying over the shoulder, better known by the name of 'follow me, lads' and such like decoys, are unmistakably intended to attract the notice and attention of the male sex.

Letter to *The Times*, 1862

It is ... alarming, peculiarly at this time when impressing upon us woman's general missionariness to see that dress of women is daily unfitting them for any 'mission' or usefulness at all ... Compelled by her dress, every woman now either shuffles or waddles ... the fidget of silk and of crinoline, the crackling of starched petticoats, ... the creaking of stays and shoes ... Her skirts (and well if they do not throw down some piece of furniture) will at least brush against every article in the room as she moves ... Fortunate is she if she does not catch fire.

Florence Nightingale, *Notes on Nursing*, 1859

1865–1880

The period between 1865 and 1880 was one of intellectual and social ferment, accompanied by a deepening economic depression. Paris remained the international fashion centre despite France's defeat in the Franco-Prussian War, the fall of Napoleon III and the replacement of the Second Empire by the Third Republic.

Initially, ladies' fashions were ebullient, extrovert and extravagant:

And sometimes, as at this present moment, it is in oddity, in the widest extremes and the most startling changes. Emphatically, we do not know what a day may bring forth in the way of toilet. When we go to bed we leave our wives and daughters in huge bell-shaped crinolines, breaking jugs, upsetting chairs, damaging their male neighbours' shins, and showing their own legs with a liberality of which the funniest thing is that every lady sees and deprecates the same display in others, but ignores it stoutly for herself; when we wake up the next morning they are in narrow, close-sitting garments, like spill boxes instead of bells. One day they have trains eddying round their feet like ghosts' garments, the next they are in short and scanty costume dresses more like pillow-cases than conventional gowns.

The Saturday Review, 1868

... we went ... to consult a *couturière en vogue* ... she opened an album of historical costumes, ... 'This is where I now get all my ideas from for new toilets. Fashions ... never were in such a vague state as they are now. Each lady comes to ask me not *what is worn* but what has not yet ever been seen or worn ... Their dream is to possess something more beautiful and more strange than was ever seen before ... my inventive powers would be inadequate ... so I open my album of historical costumes and copy ... the *marquises* of the Pompadour period, the *grande dame* of the Louis XIV court or, still further back, the pretty adornments of La Belle Gabrielle or Diane de Poitiers'.

Englishwoman's Domestic Magazine, 1868

From the mid-1870s fashions become apparently much more severe, but:

To hide yet to display, or rather to indicate and yet disclose, are the two objects of the bodice . . . It must not be forgotten that often what is concealed is just that which is most wished to be displayed. The significance of the bodice results from this fact.

Charles Blanc, *Art and Ornament*, 1875 English Edition, 1877

The extravagance of the early period is modified increasingly by a need for economy:

the washing silk . . . for any gaiety, such as an archery or garden party . . . I should advise that this be black and white, . . . it will then answer the purpose of a demi-toilette dinner dress. Have the front made V-shaped, so that it may be easily tucked back for evening wear, and worn either with or without a simple chemisette of tulle or plaited net; also if made with a polonaise or upper skirt, it will make a change and look well, over either the black or coloured silk skirt.

A Lady, How to Dress on £15 per year, 1878

. . . I couldn't have believed a dyed dress could have turned out so well . . . four years ago . . . it did admirably as a white dinner dress, then dyed a pretty red; and now it comes out once more ever beautiful and new, black! Even the way it was made at first (1878) very full princesse with a set in train suits for the present panier style.

Mary Reed Bobbitt, *With Dearest Love to All!*
The life & letters of Lady Jebb, letter of 1882
(The author, an American married to a Cambridge Don, was not poor, and was fashion conscious.)

Reasonable Dress . . . £100 a year. I have to dress . . . out of that amount, having to be ready for about fifteen balls a season. I calculate thus – a black silk, velvet, net, and a coloured silk each with low and square-cut bodice, answers for dinners and balls . . . and with lace flounces, shawls, scarves or sashes may be made to look quite different year by year. A black silk (about £17) will serve for two seasons, being turned into dinner, ball, and evening dresses, successively afterwards. Two silk and cashmere (or fashionable material) costumes, each with high and square-cut bodices, are useful for afternoon and evening dresses alternatively; while an Ulster and plain dress, with a soft felt hat to match, are suitable for driving tours, picnics, and excursions . . . My plan is to buy dress patterns at 5s to 8s each, cut out and fit on my dresses, sending them with directions and trimmings, to a woman to complete at 10s the dress . . . In linen . . . employing poor people who owe me money to work off their debts; or women who would occasionally have to be helped, work at it when unemployed by others . . .

The Queen, 1878

Inspiration came from the couture via magazine and the stage:

. . . I am waiting myself to make my winter coat and dress until I can see the Bazaar again. At the Theatre Français they wear the most magnificent dresses I ever saw in my life . . . Sarah Bernhardt looked lovely . . . whatever I see her in, I always make up my mind to try to remember how it was made and to have one like it for myself.

Mary Reed Bobbitt, *op cit.*, letter of 1879

and of course, from magazines:

The white damask . . . is a perfect beauty . . . The enclosed picture is the design I followed for the front, taking the other part from a white satin wedding dress in another number of the Bazaar.

Mary Reed Bobbitt, *op cit.*, letter of 1880

Uniformity becomes noticeable:

Is not fashion in dress after all the outward distinction between the upper middle and lower grades of society? . . . Does not the thought of a new dress made according to the latest modes of fashion, induce Sally, the housemaid and Julia, the cook, to work harder that they may the sooner be able to ape their mistress to such an extent, that visitors are frequently at a loss to know which is the servant and which is the mistress? But, cruel fashion soon consigns Julia and Sally to the chamber and the kitchen, for as soon as the modes they have adopted become common, new ones are propounded and adopted by the mistress.

The Draper, 1871

More women turn to ready-to-wear:

. . . It is very pleasant to have a dress pretty and well-fitting for that price, a dress ready to put on, and no long bills for trimming and those dreadful sundries we all know something of.

Englishwoman's Domestic Magazine, 1869,
referring to Mrs Addley Bourne, 37 Piccadilly,
and her stock of ready made summer dresses

They also embarked on home dressmaking:

Catalogue of Patterns: Home Dressmaking either with or without the assistance of a professional dressmaker, has become so general in these days that patterns which were formerly exclusively used by a limited class, have become a public necessity. To meet the demand for really reliable patterns, which has so suddenly sprung into existence, we have, at considerable trouble and expense, arranged for a constant supply of Original and Fashionable Designs of such Costumes, Children's Dresses, Articles of

Underlinen &c, as will be most acceptable to the majority of home workers.

R. Munroe, *Practical Dressmaking*, 1879

Sewing machines and their users became more efficient. As additional attachments were devised, so styles became more complicated and trimmings increasingly ingenious:

It is certainly to be suspected that we owe much of the over-trimming now prevalent to the facilities afforded by the sewing machines, which have become valued little friends in many a household.

Sylvia, *The Lady's Guide to Home Dressmaking and Millinery*, 1876/83

The trimmings for which instructions are given include:

Puffings . . . Kiltings . . . Single Box Pleats . . . Double Box Pleats . . . Triple and Quadruple Pleats . . . Feather Ruches . . . Gathered Flounces . . . Single Gathered Flounces . . . Single Gathered Ruche . . . Fluted Ruche (or Ruche à la *vieille*) . . . Fluted Flounces . . . Narrow Silk Bindings . . . Wide Silk or Velvet Bindings . . . Crossway Bands . . . Shell Quillings . . . Plain Quillings . . . Leaf Trimming . . . Upright Puffs . . . Twisted Ruche . . . Feather Ruche . . . Gathering or Frillings . . . Braid . . . Fringing . . . Gauging . . . Quilting . . . False Buttonholes.

R. Munroe, *Practical Dressmaking*, 1879

Embroidery and beadwork were also executed by machine from the mid-1870s and this became a popular ready-made trimming, usually in a colour which matched or harmonised with the dress:

Patterns are in raised silk work and have quite the appearance of being done by hand though this of course is not the case.

Englishwoman's Domestic Magazine, 1865

The whole front covered with white bead braid and bead fringes which gleam and shine and move and give an altogether brilliant effect.

Mary Reed Bobbitt, *op cit.*, letter of 1875

The cut of the dress changed in the later 1860s as the line became less full:

Dresses incline more and more to the Princess Shape. All the widths are gored, the skirt is scant and short in front and forms a long sweeping train at the back. The body is plain with a round waist.

Englishwoman's Domestic Magazine, 1865

Overskirts accumulate and are concentrated at the rear:

Since skirts are so gored that there remains no material to pleat around the waistband . . . this style has been found unbecoming to even the slightest figures, so aprons have become very favourite additions to both morning and afternoon dresses.

The Queen, 1866

There shall be an abundance of a crinoline or bustle or pannier or tournure (for the bunch at the back goes by a variety of names) just below the waist.

The Queen, 1868

The actual crinoline is now given up or nearly so but ladies . . . wear the tournure Duchesse of fine horsehair, disposed in several flutings to keep up the full basques and retroussis of modern costume . . .

Milliner and Dressmaker, 1872

In the early to mid-1870s, fullness diminishes and what there is moves decisively to the back:

. . . a great point . . . to have all the fullness thrown to the back and a slight dégagé tournure . . . The Louis Quinze retroussé skirt . . . ungraceful . . . giving a lady the appearance of a *paquet* . . . The gored dress, with flowing drapery at the back only . . . more becoming.

Milliner and Dressmaker and Warehouseman's Gazette, 1873

In the later 1870s and early 1880s the line straightens and becomes tighter to the figure:

It is astonishing how *la ligne* which one hears so much about, alters in shape and contour, now giving as the ideal of beauty a short waist and scant robe, now a long bodice and flowing skirt.

Milliner and Dressmaker and Warehouseman's Gazette, 1875

. . . new cuirasse bodice, which is cut low and laced at the back, and comes down quite plain over the hips so as very greatly to resemble a corset put *over* the dress instead of under.

Englishwoman's Domestic Magazine, 1875

. . . Who has not seen a gardener at work with black tight fitting jacket and white or grey sleeves? Behold the cuirass with sleeves of a different colour. Next comes the tablier or apron and sash exactly in form as those of a dishwasher.

The Ladies' Treasury, 1875

The great aim is to make the figure as flat and sheathlike as possible and upon the block to wind as close as may be all kinds of draperies.

Ibid.

. . . coming Season . . . waists worn long one and a half inches or more. This joined to the increasing tightness with which our skirts are held back will make us look even longer and slimmer than before.

Englishwoman's Domestic Magazine, 1875

The silhouette and posture change at the beginning of the 1870s when heels and hair dressing are both high:

A lady of five feet becomes say five feet two inches per heels, five feet six inches per hair, five feet again per Grecian bend.

Morning Advertisor, 1871

Coiffure

Hair dressing becomes more elaborate and curls and braids at the back are dressed progressively higher, which affects the style of the bonnet:

The fashion of wearing the hair is everyday growing more exaggerated. At the back of the head chignons bows and curls are placed *en masse* descending a considerable way down the nape of the neck.

The Queen, 1864

Bonnets ... smaller than ever ... the cap has almost entirely disappeared as well as the curtain.

Englishwoman's Domestic Magazine, 1865

The hair is worn in a plaited chignon, higher on the head than ever before.

The Queen, 1867

One day they have huge flapping hats that overshadow the shoulders, the next little 'porridge-plates' that do not come beyond the line of the hair. Now they let their tresses meander in greasy ringlets of the corkscrew shape, or hang in a heavy smooth and shining roll half-way down their necks, and moëlline and macassar make a man's fortune out of hand; and now they puff it out in big cushions on the top of their heads, and resort to artificial means to make it crinkly, dry, and absolutely without gloss.

The Saturday Review, 1868

In town ... the Tyrolese hat ... The fashion was first sported by gentlemen who copied it exactly from the Tyrolese peasants ... the ladies ... wear them excessively small ... of soft grey felt, and vary the trimming ... in general it is formed of wide ribbon and an aigrette of ... feathers (worn) on the top of their heads very much forward, without attempting to make them fit ... next to the Tyrolese, the tricorne hat is most in favour.

Englishwoman's Domestic Magazine, 1869

The hair being now raised higher than ever at the top of the head, though now dropping very low down in the neck, there can be no material change in the shape of the bonnets which still occupy but a very small space upon the front of the head, leaving all the back of it and the ears entirely uncovered ... the bonnet ... is fast disappearing ... reduced to a mere diadem.

Ibid.

A general rule ... is that the bonnet is put very much at the top of the head, so as to cover all the hair behind and leaving nearly all the top of the head uncovered. This fashion has brought about a change in hair-dressing, for ... the hair is therefore now brought down very much lower over the brow in frizzles or in undulations called '*dents*' which come down over the forehead, sometimes to the eyebrows, but that is certainly not becoming. It cannot but strike one very much this change in the style of the coiffure.

Englishwoman's Domestic Magazine, 1875

The round *marin anglais* hat with sloped up brim all round ... is a great favourite with ladies of almost all ages. These chapeaux are exactly the same shape as our little boys' felt hats ... only they are ornamented with feathers and aigrettes and tied with broad strings of ... ribbon.

Ibid.

Outerwear

As the line becomes more form fitting, jackets replace shawls and mantles for outerwear.

... the mannish woman – the woman who wears a double-breasted coat with big buttons, of which she flings back the lappels, with an air, understanding the suggestiveness of a wide chest and the need of unchecked breathing; who wears unmistakable shirtfronts, linen collars, vests and plain ties, like a man ...

The Saturday Review, 1868

The Dolman which is now so fashionable is ... nothing but a short paletot with very wide hanging sleeves ... made mostly of cloth ... useful ... as an extra mantle to be donned over the *costume complet* when the day is cold.

Milliner and Dressmaker and Warehouseman's Gazette, 1872

Mantles and jackets were usually bought ready to wear but since they tended to be expensive, their style may lag behind the rest of the outfit:

It was not necessary to have a new jacket every year. If one has a sealskin and a good tailor made cloth jacket in one's wardrobe, they will wear for years.

Sylvia, *The Lady's Guide to Home Dressmaking*, 1876/83

Colours were rich at the beginning of the period:

Lyons ... some of the new materials prepared for the winter ... ribbed velvets, ... striped tissues, ... The favourite colours are golden pheasant, garnet, plum colour, ruby, marine blue, reddish purple, lavender ... Vesuvius red, Orient grey and a deep orange ... For the evening ... beautiful poult-de-soie, pale blue, orange, mauve or pearl-grey shot with white ...

Englishwoman's Domestic Magazine, 1869

to be succeeded by lighter, prettier pastels and an increased use of light trimmings:

A faille dress of pale nenuphar green, with thick watered stripes, is also very elegant ... a tunic tied at the back with a wide sash to match ... it had a postillion basque at the back with wide box-plaits, and shorter basques in front. It was trimmed *en chale* with Alençon lace arranged over a wide black velvet band ...

The Queen, 1872

Underwear

Despite the form-fitting outline, underwear was traditional and utilitarian for the greater part of the period.

Your wardrobe ... of underlinen ... you have a sufficiency of shifts in good order, but your drawers are only so-so; and as to nightdresses, you will have to get some at once ... You are pretty well set up in petticoats ... you have three or four good calico, and a muslin one for evening wear, a couple of coloured ones and a strong linsey ... an evening crinoline, besides the one you are wearing every day, and a pair of cleaned stays ...

A Lady, How to Dress on £15 per year, circa 1878

While crinolines (even the half round versions of the earlier 1870s) were worn, corsetting was less important:

Stays and crinolines ... The former have of late become very reasonable. The French woven stay, or, what is slighter still, a riding belt, will be quite sufficient support for an ordinary figure, and cost from half-a-crown to five shillings ... an excellent plan to make a thin calico loose cover, to be tacked on, so that it can constantly be taken off and washed; ... the stays will not require cleaning so frequently, which is apt to spoil the shape.

Crinolines ... of a very good quality for five shillings ... Those with gingham or mohair covering are better than those covered with calico, which soon gets cut at the bottom by the steel. It is a good plan to save the list of flannel and tack it on the bottom steel, laying on that again a piece of strong tape; by this means you will prevent the sharp edge of the steel from cutting through the material, and also from injuring your boots.

Ibid.

Legs and feet are less of a feature in the 1870s than in the previous or succeeding decade:

Footwear
Stockings should be carefully chosen to suit your petticoat or dress. Dark indigo blue and dark brown are amongst the best wearing colours. Greys and drabs, especially in cotton, are apt to fade, and become after a few washings of a dirty white or yellow ... You would get cotton and thread for summer, and merino for winter use ... I should recommend plain colours, as striped stockings are very apt to wear unequally, and give where the stripes meet. Thread are the prettiest of all; ... but they are rather expensive – about four shillings a pair – whereas you will get cotton at two shillings, or thereabouts ... Spun silk is very pleasant to wear, but very extravagant; they cost from six and sixpence to eight or nine shillings a pair, and run into holes very quickly.

Ibid.

For boots ... for those who are not very particular about their appearance, and walk little, thin boots and goloshes are the most economical, though certainly not becoming ... Cashmere boots can be bought good and strong for three and sixpence ...

Nice shoes need not cost more than two and sixpence, and these, with a bow, made up of any old scrap of ribbon, and set off with good steel buckles, will always look nice.

Ibid.

Accessories
In regard to gloves ... for town ... kid in summer, and for the winter double sewn calf or dog-skin ... Black, with coloured or white sewn backs, are good wear; dark purple is an excellent wearing colour, though not pretty ... For a country life, untanned garden gauntlets are the most suitable. Pale grey and yellow kid gloves can always be worn at night and look better than white ...

Ibid.

... he gave me ... an immense painted black satin fan for my birthday. These big fans are all the fashion in London, nobody carries anything else.

Mary Reed Bobbit, *op cit.*, letter of 1874

Make up seems to be acceptable even in middle class circles:

I think my readers must have gone a little mad upon the subject of their *eyelashes*, for I have had so many letters upon the possibility of darkening and improving them ... Now I would counsel that those who require, or who fancy they require, beautifying, to purchase the CASKET OF BEAUTY, an elegant box containing the following necessaries in this agreeable art:– one box kohl, one eyebrow pencil, one pot snow-white cream, one pot Hebe bloom, one box perline, one box velveteen, one pot lip-salve, one bottle lotion, one cosmetique, one box glycerine – ten articles, the whole free from metallic paint or other injurious ingredients. The 'Casket of Beauty' is sold at 21s.

Englishwoman's Domestic Magazine, 1874

Late 1870s–1890s

Visible distinction between classes slowly begins to become less apparent in the last two decades of the century:

There is still some difference so far as dress is concerned between a gentleman's groom and a gentleman but there is absolutely none, apart from the material, between the attire of a housemaid on her 'day out' and that of her mistress and were the two to be photographed in one frame it might be hard to tell which was the lady and which the domestic.

Warehousemen and Drapers' Trade Gazette, 1876,
quoting from *The Telegraph*

As economic depression begins to lift, purchasing power increases and with the increasing availability of ready to wear clothing comes a greater general uniformity of dress type and variety of accessories.

Communications improve and shops become larger. Department stores such as William Whiteley of Bayswater expand but fashion inspiration is still French:

[Whiteley's] Costume Ball and Evening Dress Department Entrances Nos 43, 49 & 51 Westbourne Grove. A MAGNIFICENT Saloon running in the rear of the whole range of shops ... and without doubt the largest Costume Show Room in the world, has been wholly devoted to this Department. The Paris houses are continually visited, and all the latest novelties carefully selected ...

The system permitted individuality combined with economy. Whiteley's dressmaking department aimed to

... combine the utmost elegance of style and execution with the lowest possible charges.
Catalogue of William Whiteley, Universal Providor, circa 1885

The stage also affected fashion:

The production of a new play in any of the leading theatres in Paris is always an occasion for the display of new costumes and criticisms on the dress worn by the chief artistes are as important as are those on the play itself. The dresses then first seen are eagerly examined, admired, censured but most assuredly copied whatever the verdict may be.
Myra's Journal, 1881

The standard of education for women rose and as their horizons expanded, so did expectations and opportunities – the 'New Woman' of the late nineteenth century is much more sporty and extrovert than her predecessors:

Girls now have a full fine life opening before them ... The girl of today, with her fine physical development, her bright cheery nature ... has a vigorous contempt for all forms of softness; her mind and character are strung up to a firmness of which a sentimental heroine of fifty years ago would have been ashamed. She is a good comrade with her brothers, sharing most of their sports and pastimes. Her chief accomplishments are waltzing and tennis.
C. Willett Cunnington, quoting from an unstated source in *Feminine Attitudes in the 19th Century*

Her choice of wardrobe tended to polarise formal and elaborate as against tailored every day toilettes:

The contrast between plain and elaborate toilettes has never been greater than at present. Though many dresses now worn are in the simplest styles but display the most perfect make and completeness in all details ... very rich materials are often used for visiting and promenade dresses to be worn in the afternoon.
Myra's Journal, 1882

A tailormade gown ... is suited to almost all occasions when morning dress is permissible. Such costumes are worn in London at the smartest weddings and afternoon parties, and would not be out of place in a long country walk across stubble fields or for a tour abroad.
Woman's World, 1889

This we have at least the grace to encourage from year to year ... the coat and skirt worn with shirt or blouse.
Sylvia's Home Journal, 1893

During the 1870s and 1880s alternative modes of dress were chosen by those, following the Pre-Raphaelites, who found fashionable styles unattractive or unhealthy. By 1884, the year of the International Health Exhibition, the demand for 'reform' dress was such that the London shop, Liberty's opened a new department, supervised by the architect and designer E. W. Goodwin (1833–86), devoted to 'A New School of Dressmaking'. Its aim was to:

... re-establish the craft upon some hygenic, intelligible and progressive basis; to initiate a renaissance ... which would commend itself to leaders of art and fashion to challenge ... Paris for 'change' and 'novelty' in so far as it was oblivious of grace and fitness.

Average aesthetic dress tended to:

The puffed sleeves, the aesthetic skirts, the naïve adornments of bead and shell, the formless hat ... 'after Gainsborough'.
Mrs Humphrey Ward describing Rose, the musical 'Miss Artistic' in *Robert Elsemere,* 1888

Aesthetic comfort and fashionable tastes meet in the creation of a new garment, the 'teagown', the informal indoor dress, flowing, loose fitting, and necessitating no corsets. This was suited to the slightly less formal pattern of social life which developed towards the end of the century:

Twenty years ago [a woman had] ... a morning dress, a visiting dress, a low necked dinner dress, and a ball gown, the number ... decided by individual requirements. Now women dress for dinner in ... many different ways ... Low gowns, half-high gowns or tea-gowns ... akin to dressing gowns or tea-gowns ... inspired by the modes of mediaeval times ... you have to know the habits of your host and hostess when you pack you trunk.
Woman's World, 1889

The cut began to change with the new decade:

There had beside been a complete transformation in the method of draping skirts, the *jupe* itself being now made perfectly flat, with a large tablier ending in a series of puffs at the back, very much raised and fussily arranged.
Myra's Journal, 1882

This back emphasis was to develop supported on bustles or 'tournures', which are readvertised:

tournures are now quite re-established amongst us, as might have been expected when the full draperies ar the back were adopted ... Crinoline and red Turkey cotton are the matterials used ...

The Queen, 1881

Then the rounded lines straighten and the trimming simplifies:

All elaborate frillings and puffings are fast disappearing in favour of straight, falling lines. The under-skirt is now often completely hidden except at some point where the square apron or tunic is raised at one side.

Lady's World, 1886

A taste for asymmetry develops:

Skirts now never have two sides alike.

Lady's World, 1887

Change is imminent when:

... The 'bustle' is doomed and the lines of the skirt are simpler and longer ... waists are growing shorter.

Woman's World, 1887–88

For the 1890s, interest shifts from skirt to bodice:

It matters little how plain the skirt is; the bodice is all-important; and for dressy occasions full vests and jabots are almost a necessity.

Woman's World, 1889

The emphasis is now on the sleeve, which is set higher at the shoulder and becomes much larger:

What can be more ludicrous than the present fashion of irrelevant and enormous sleeves.

Woman's World, 1890

Changing its form:

... sleeves are no longer made immoderately high at the shoulder; the upper part is usually more or less draped at the top, but the latest idea is to bring drapery down to the elbow.

The Lady's Magazine, 1892

And by the autumn:

The newest sleeves are immense, especially those of plain shot velvet.

Ibid.

There is a short lived vogue, rather more French than English, for 'The Empire Line'. This appears in Paris in 1890:

The Empire craze ... pretty Empire frocks of last season were only the first few drops of an avalanche ... Some have the short bodice of last season ... but for the greater part are long Princess dresses falling from a long yoke.

Ibid.

The skirt at first is tight to the figure:

Skirts are nearly all gored, clinging closely to the figure, except at the back, where they flow outwards in a slight train.

Ibid.

A new inspiration coalesces the developing lines of the dress:

... every novelty in skirt, bodice or sleeve is traceable to the study of fashion plates issued between 1827–31. The leg-of-mutton sleeve reigns supreme ... The skirt is beginning to flow outwards as it nears the ground, instead of clinging to the limbs.

Ibid.

This development is confirmed when:

Worth has just brought out a skirt fitted at the waist, but over seven yards wide at the lower edge.

The Lady's Magazine, 1893–4

The waistline is also affected:

... the bodice round-waisted with a belt or a small corselet of some description, or else it has long basques.

Fashion, 1893

In the second half of the decade the line begins to lengthen, the inspiration changing from Regency to sixteenth century:

The Louis Onze period calls for long slender waists and will necessitate a drastic change in our corsets. Square-cut bodices, filled up with full chemisettes ... and Viennese funnel collars or stiff ruffles will be closely adhered to ... We do not know where collars are going to stop ...

The Woman at Home, 1896

The sleeve diminishes:

But the chief change noticeable for the last month is the attempt to diminish or at least flatten down the width of sleeves.

Ibid.

Emphasis shifts to the bodice instead by means of boleros or bolero effects which:

appears on nearly every dress either for morning or evening wear, and in every variety of material from velvet to lace.

The Graphic, 1897

And:

All fullness has vanished save at the shoulder where pointed and square epaulettes, puffs or butterfly arrangements maintain their wide effect which makes the waist look small.

Ibid.

A new line is confirmed by a choice of new materials:

All clinging materials will be used and even cloth will be of a soft texture.

The Lady's Realm, 1898–99

Everything is veiled or trimmed with chiffon, jewelled net, the flimsiest of gauzes with tuckings, gaugings and pleatings.

The Lady's Realm, 1898

By the end of the century, the line is smooth and fitting but much more rounded:

Monaco Dec. 15th 1899 ... You ought to see the skirts, not a wave of fullness anywhere, but such proportions as these French women show! No artificial tournures required. The skirt is held tightly with one hand across the lower back to keep the slight train off the ground; ...

Mary Reed Bobbitt, *op cit.*, letter of 1899

Coiffure

The coiffure begins to change early in the 1880s, though slowly and hesitantly:

... great change in style of coiffure ... the expressionless fringe is giving place to the waved bandeau ... classic knot becoming a thing of the past. The new coiffure follows the line of the head but less closely.

Myra's Journal, 1881–82

The back hair is knotted high on the crown until *circa* 1895 when it slips down to midway. The later 1890s hairstyles become softer:

Quite a series of new hair dressings ... a soft aureole of narrow waves and curls, brushed back in rippling wavelets over the forehead ...

The Woman at Home, 1896

Hats are plain and worn tilted forward at the crown. Sailor hats become and continue to be popular for informal occasions:

The hats which are distinctly new have brims that widen in front and more closely resemble the sailor shape than any other. Some of these brims turn upwards like an inverted saucer.

Woman's World, 1888

Hairstyles in turn affected the shape of hats:

Trimming is no longer a feature of our millinery; the hats are large, wide and rather floppy, to suit the present style of hair-dressing which is wilder than ever.

The Woman at Home, 1896

Underwear

The slim figure necessitated by the close fitting lines was achieved by rigid corsetry:

The Specialité Corset (Registered No 10438). The advantages secured by the wearer ... are as follows:– ... manufactured under scientific supervision, the cut and make being perfect; each bone is placed in the position requiring support, without impeding or checking the proper exercise of the muscles, allowing perfect freedom of action to the whole frame; all these advantages are obtained with an additional elegance of form ... ladies preferring a long graceful waist will find Models 1 and 2 perfect ... fitted throughout with *Real Whalebone* (Busks and Side Steels excepted).

Dickins and Jones, Regent Street, W1. Complete Wedding Outfitters (Catalogue) *circa* 1890

The rounded contours of the end of the century required a new form of corset, in intention less restrictive:

straight fronted ... cut low ... so that an absolutely natural appearance is preserved at the bust, but its leading characteristic is a perfectly straight busk which keeps the figure flat in front below the waist.

The Queen, 1900

No fashionable woman needs tight lace; she is required to present an unbroken line from the decolletage to the knee and this prevents any undue drawing in of the waist line.

The Queen, 1901

and a simplification of underwear:

'Shocked?' 'Why?' 'Well, I hardly like to tell you: but the fact is, that I have so little on'. 'I don't wear much', said the other. 'All I have is combination, stays and one petticoat under my dress' ... They passed for two of the best-dressed girls at the fashionable watering-place where we were staying.

Ada S. Ballin, *The Science of Dress*, 1885

New and more clinging fabrics became fashionable for underwear:

Woven combinations ... the combinations being made in a stretchy material, fit somewhat closely and show the symmetry of the figure.

Ibid.

... increasing in favour ... The silken undergarments, ... trimmed with white or black lace ... very short, very full ... each set of the same exact shade of colour ... made in delicate pink, blue, white, maize, red and in black especially. The stays are of satin of the same shade.

Woman's World, 1888

It was impossible to walk or sit in such tightly fitted dresses without showing the foot and ankle, so that stockings and shoes became a fashion feature:

Highly decorated stockings ... small palms woven ... beaded ... with sprays embroidered in black and white, gold and velvet and gold.

The Queen, 1881

Accessories

The new taste for tailored clothes led to the introduction of new accessories:

We borrow our fashions from various sources ...

now we have turned to boatmen and adopted their jerseys ... They are difficult to get into, for they have no opening and are seamless, consequently they must be pulled over the head: they are trying to any but a perfect figure, for they fit as closely as silk glove or stocking ... but, notwithstanding, for lawn tennis, yachting and archery, fashionable women have made them a current mode.

The Queen, 1879

Blouses have grown so much in popular favour ... that from *négligé* garments of the loosest, baggiest, and most unpretentious description they have developed into the favourite bodices of the age ...

Woman's World, 1890

... the 'Henley' stiff-fronted shirt was also introduced, and was eagerly sought after by the masculine girl ... Then the vital distinction between a blouse and a shirt was in the matter of these same collars and cuffs; if stiff the garment was a shirt – if soft, it was a blouse ...

The Draper's World: Sixty Years of Fashion,
1837–97, 1897

Colours
Colours were sombre and rich at the beginning of the period with a preference for maroons and browns contrasting with greens and yellows but in the last decade could become much brighter with sharper contrasts:

The most incongruous mixtures are worn in one gown ... a dress of prune hopsack canvas. The bodice opens on a square of fawn satin cloth with tiny spots of prune ... revers ... finished with a bow of geranium velvet ... studded with tiny diamond-shaped garnet buttons.

... the favourite combinations being white, buff, or a deep red on navy blue; brick red, royal blue, or fawn with dark green; blue ... amber or petunia or brown.

The Woman at Home, 1896

With the variety of clothing available, there was stress on specialised garments such as those for the new popular athletic pursuits.

Tricycling
Neat, dark cloth costumes, ulsters or jackets, with small felt or cloth hats to match, are suitable for tricycle wear, or dresses of those brownish materials which do not show the dust of the road ... The dress worn by the members of the Ladies' Cyclist Touring Club is made of dark grey tweed, and consists of a Norfolk jacket, a long skirt covering knickerbockers, and a hat to match ... Tight-lacing must be banished from the mind and body of the woman who would ride the iron steed ...

Ada S. Ballin, op cit., 1885

Cycling
Is it the cycling craze or is it the travelling season which has brought in such a shoal of examples of the Norfolk jacket? The Norfolk jacket adheres to its three pleat back and front ... generally made in tweed. It is not a style for elegant materials.

The Lady's Magazine, 1892

Tennis
Messrs Redfern and Son of Cowes and Conduit Street ... tennis dress of pure English wool ... made of serge, with two kilt flounces, so arranged that, while the skirt gives ample scope for the movement ... the kiltings keep their places; the Jersey bodice, made of fine English wool elastic cloth, is finished off with a scarf tunic turned upwards and forming two pockets for the ball.

The Queen, 1881

Riding
Many improvements have taken place of late in ladies' dress for horse exercise. The long habits ... were alike objectionable and dangerous; ... The skirt should not be longer than just to cover the feet, and the material chosen should be as light as possible ... For riding, as for other exercise, the body should be clothed in wool. The habit should invariably be lined with flannel ... all the underclothing that is required is woollen combinations with perhaps the belt as described, or the belt and stays in the case of those inclined to *enbonpoint*.

Ada S. Ballin, op cit., 1885

Mourning
Ritual mourning dress was becoming somewhat démodé with the upper classes in the 1880s, and was, by their betters, considered extravagant in the lower classes but its conventions were still observed by the respectable majority of the community:

... generally ... the terms and degrees of mourning which are sanctioned by custom as being usual and sufficient ... The first degree of mourning is ... that of a widow; the dress is always of paramatta entirely covered with crape to within an inch or two of the waist, the crape being in one piece, not in separate tucks, for the first nine months ... after this period ... it may be put on in two deep tucks, with about an inch space between them, but must come up as high on the skirt as before. The sleeves are tight to the arm, the body entirely covered with crape, and deep lawn cuffs and collar are worn. The cap was formerly constructed so as almost entirely to conceal the hair and to fasten under the chin; but ... now ... many different shapes are worn, the Marie Stuart ... being the most general. It must be worn for a year and a day. The outdoor dress has a jacket or mantle of paramatta very heavily trimmed with crape; ... The bonnet is entirely crape, with a widow's cap tacked inside it, and with a crape veil with a deep hem ... After ... silk, heavily trimmed with crape, may be worn for six months, after which the crape can be considerably lessened, and jet trimmings used to brighten the toilette ... after two years mourning may be laid aside, though it is much better taste to wear half-mourning for at least six months more. The next degree of mourning is that of a child for a parent or a parent for a child ... The period ... is twelve months, and for the first paramatta heavily trimmed with crape, and with lawn collars and cuffs is worn ... A crape bonnet with jet ornament or a black feather ... for the first three months. After that time silk may be worn with, ... rather less crape ... After six months, crape is laid aside, ... After nine months, half-mourning is permissible ... A wife wears mourning for her husband's parents, or any of his other relatives precisely as she would for her own ... The orthodox period of mourning for brother or sister is six months, of which three must be in crape, two in black, and one in half-mourning; for grandparents nine months – three in crape, three in black, three in half-mourning. Three months for an uncle, or aunt, nephew or niece. No crape is requisite ... Two months are sufficient for a great uncle or aunt. For first cousins the period is six weeks, three of which may be slight, and three weeks are sufficient for a second cousin, though, indeed, mourning is very frequently omitted ... for so distant a relation ... These cases, I think, exhaust the list of absolute relationship ... It is the fashion to abuse mourning, to shorten by every pretence the period of wearing it, and more especially to complain of crape ... to curtail the period of mourning ... many members of the English upper classes are drifting slowly in the same direction, ...

The Lady's Guide to Home Dressmaking and Millinery, 1876/83

Children's dress

Those who were children in the reign of Queen Victoria rarely regarded their clothing with affection, to judge from retrospective accounts. Perhaps it was because they were conscious that fashionable dress was what parents wanted and had little to do with what children liked or needed. Throughout the period they had the dress reformers on their side:

In these days of elaboration and extravagance in dress, children are too frequently seen dressed out in imitation of grown-up persons, like miniatures reproducing on a small scale each detail of puff, frill, furbelow and manufactured protruberance ... Children's clothes should be of simple material ... simply made ... It is not ... the wealthiest people who dress their children most elaborately. It is the nouveaux riches, ...

The Lady's Guide to Home Dressmaking and Millinery, 1876/83

Boys suffered less from fashionable constraints than girls who endured the entire adult style sequence from long tight bodices through corsets, crinolines,

bustles, and big sleeves all more or less scaled down to juvenile size.

The boys ... their dress did not offer the slightest restraint on their freedom of movement. It was otherwise with the girls ... they were dressed in low dresses, and their shoulders were so bare that we involuntarily thought of a caterpillar casting its skin ... when we realised that this was rendered impossible by the tightness of the clothes about the waist ... it entirely destroyed their freedom of movement.

Mrs Merrifield, *The Art of Dress*, 1854

Those persons who, like myself can remember the dress of little girls thirty or forty years ago will recollect that even at that time all girls wore low frocks fastened behind, and short sleeves, and when they went out of doors they put on a pelisse or a spencer, or a tippet and sleeves. No child, except those of quite the higher classes wore drawers, or trousers as they were called, and all stays laced behind, and had a busk of steel for grown people and generally wood for girls.

Englishwoman's Domestic Magazine, 1874

Come the little ones in frocks,
With their broidered knickerbocks,
And their tangled sunny locks,
Laughing crew.

Come the dimpled darling pets,
With their tresses all in nets,
And their snow-white pantalettes,
Full in view.

Come the gay and graceful girls,
With their chignons and their curls,
Sweetest string of beauty's pearls,
Two and Two.

J. Ashby-Sterry, *Two and Two*, probably late 1860s–1870s

... my gowns, petticoats, crinolines, ribbons, ties, cloaks, hats, bonnets, gloves, capes, hooks, eyes, buttons and the hundred and one etceteras that make a girl's costume.

Helen Mathers, *Comin' Through the Rye*, circa 1870

Fabrics tend to be somewhat miscellaneous because in the thrifty household it was common practice to unpick and re-use garments to make children's clothes. Despite this some fabrics and forms of decoration are more noticeable in this context:

Although plaid materials are no longer much employed for ladies dresses, they are still generally chosen for children's costumes.

Englishwoman's Domestic Magazine, 1864

Frocks and capes for young children are more than ever arranged for braiding, no other ornament having as yet been found so suitable for the purpose.

Ibid.

Smocking so popular one or two years ago for lawn tennis costume has now found its way into children's dress.

The Queen, 1880

The sort of clothing worn is affected by the age of the child. The categories are similar to those we observe today; infants, the first few months of life; babies, to walking stage; young children, to about five years of age; boys became 'young gentlemen' at about thirteen or fourteen; girls became 'young ladies', at about sixteen or seventeen.

Babies

Babies were dressed in layers of flannel and cotton in an attempt to combine warmth and washability:

Infants for the first three or four months are clothed in very long petticoats . . . they help to keep the feet of the infant safe from cold air, which would otherwise chill an infant very severely, and long clothes do also give a nurse a good hold of a child, who without sufficient clothing would be apt to slip out of her arms.

Thomas Webster, FGS, assisted by the late Mrs Parkes, *An Encyclopaedia of Domestic Economy*, 1844

Slowly, simplicity infiltrated:

. . . caps, with their trimmings of three or four rows of lace and large cockades which rivalled in size the dear little round face of the child, are discontinued almost entirely indoors.

Mrs Merrifield, *The Art of Dress*, 1854

Babies' outfits were numerous and could be expensive and elaborate, but:

Almost any amount of money may be spent on the decoration of the various articles of an infant's clothing. Embroidery and lace are both lavishly used . . . We would advise young mother's to avoid needless display . . . The clothing *absolutely necessary* . . . 6 Nightdresses 6 Day ditto 24 Diapers 4 Long flannels 4 Flannel squares (pilches) 2 Common head-flannels 1 Best ditto 1 Large flannel shawl 3 Robes 2 Macintosh pilches 4 Plain frocks 4 Long petticoats 6 Bibs 1 Cloak 1 Hood . . . 3 Pairs woollen boots Binders . . .

Cassell's Household Guide, circa 1880

The greatest alteration that has been made for some time regards the length of the little one's dress. Robes that once reached absurd proportions are curtailed to the length of a yard and the yard may even include the bodice . . . the body including the band is two and a half inches more than the old ones.

Ibid.

THE BABY'S CLOAK – It has been very usual lately and more fashionable to drape a baby in a simple deep circular cape out of doors, in preference to the old cloak with its cape . . . Two yards of cashmere . . . is required. White is the most esteemed

and scarlet the most durable, of colours . . . very pretty . . . white cashmere, trimmed with bright, light blue llama . . . Up the front several handsome ribbon bows . . . and the cloak secured beneath them by hooks and eyes . . . may be lined throughout with white sarcenet; but it is very general, and far less costly to use fine white cambric.

Ibid.

The dress of boy babies differed slightly from that of girls:

Don't they dress them pretty much alike? Pretty considerably so, but not exactly. You see, Sir, boys has rosettes in the cap, and girls has not.

Extract from a short story in
The Ladies' Treasury, 1858

At about the age of six months, babies were 'short coated'.

Short frocks, or, as they are called, three-quarter frocks, which are first used for babies, measure about half a yard long in the skirt, . . . After a month or two, a few more tucks are run in these skirts, to enable a child to walk freely . . . Plain muslin . . . quite sufficient . . . but where it is desired to have them handsomer . . . they may be made like long frocks as regards the embroidery . . . many mothers use pretty light fine-printed cambrics or white pique; or in winter merino, or plaid. . . . In winter . . . a pelisse made exactly like a frock with a high body and long sleeves, and a cape and collar below . . . the waist. Black velveteen, grey or blue merino are very suitable . . . Trim . . . a broad military braid . . . quilted silk . . . white worsted braid . . . fur . . . Ruby velveteen trimmed with grey imitation chinchilla fur is a very handsome mixture. To match . . . the head-dress for a girl is a little drawn bonnet of the same material edged with fur; while for a boy a little round cap or hat is suitable.

Cassell's Household Guide, circa 1880

Boys

Little boys can only be distinguished from girls by details of dress and accessory. Petticoats for boys had generations of justification and 'pantalettes', the dangling drawers of the 1850s and early 1860s tend to confuse the issue. On the whole boys tend to have less bunchy skirts, belts or girdles and additional button trim and different headgear, hats not bonnets. As they got older, their dresses merged with tunics and these became blouses which fastened at the front. Village boys wore smocks until about the 1880s.

[Leonard, going visiting had] a cap on his head, a scarlet comforter round his neck, with the ends tucked into the black belt round his sturdy waist and brown Holland blouse. His hands, with comfortable worsted gloves on, were in the pockets of his plaid trousers; but he took care that no-one should see, under the blouse that dreadful plaid tunic to match . . . If that were seen, who would ever believe that he had worn a real jacket and waistcoat every Sunday, since he was nine years old five months ago?

Charlotte M. Yonge, *Leonard The Lion Heart*, 1856

I have a little boy between 5 and 6 years of age, ... I do not like dressing children like men so young ... yet I suppose I cannot keep my boy much longer in petticoats ... I intend him to have the tunic and knickerbockers ... but do not know what he ought to wear under ... [Reply] ... make him a nice flannel shirt with longish skirts which will tuck round him nicely ... I began my boys in knickerbocker suits at 4 years old ... They had flannel shirts exactly like 'Papa', little corded stays, with buttons on which the knickerbockers buttoned ... I always tacked a pair of lining drawers inside the knickerbockers. The waistcoat was always made back and front of the same stuff, not with lining back as the tailor's do, for equal protection of the lungs. Jacket rather high, and at first had a little embroidered frill or lace collar on the velvet suits, with a blue bow; afterwards linen collars and 'grown up' ties. In summer I gave them piqué suits and holland suits, grey linen and ticking suits; in winter cloth; and in spring and autumn serge ... many of my own dresses cut up into suits, and all were made at home until the beginning of 1872 when the eldest went to boarding-school and were put into the tailor's hands.

Englishwoman's Domestic Magazine, 1874

Styles became much more stereotyped after the 1860s, the great age of the outfitter, and can be dated by comparison with adult styles. Schoolboys wore long trousers until the 1860s when knickerbockers were introduced. They were caught in at the knee. In the later 1870s these began to be replaced by shorts of the same length which continue until the end of the century. Eton and Harrow suits were worn in many less élitist establishments. Norfolk suits became increasingly popular in the 1880s and 1890s.

For younger children there were some picturesque alternatives: the Highland suit popularised by the Royal Family who wore kilts and plaids during holidays at Balmoral. Adaptable for either sex, girls wearing them with pleated skirts and boys with trousers, were the:

Sailor suits for boys and girls are just now much in vogue and will be so until the end of October.

The Ladies' Treasury, 1883

Popular with literary and artistic parents was the Fauntleroy suit, inspired by the illustration in Frances Hodgson Burnett's *Little Lord Fauntleroy*, 1885. This was said to have been copied from the kind of suit in which Mrs Burnett had dressed her son:

A graceful childish figure in a black velvet suit with a lace collar and with lovelocks waving about his handsome manly little face.

Frances Hodgson Burnett, *Little Lord Fauntleroy*, 1885

The popularisation of the jersey in the late 1870s and 1880s was a boon to children and dress reformers alike. Boys wore them with shorts and girls with pleated skirts:

Jersey costumes both for boys and girls will be more popular than ever this year; indeed these and washing dresses are the only costumes worn by children for ordinary wear ... Jersey costumes are better for boys than girls though equally comfortable for both ... Besides being very pretty they are very healthy suits; they do not impede the boys' movements ... they are cool, they admit the air, and yet being woollen they keep the body in a due state of warmth and prevent all chills.

Myra's Journal, 1884

Girls

The average girl wore a more or less fashionable frock, covered when at home with an overall or at least an apron. The styles do not differ according to age, but the length does.

A girl of sixteen writes; Mamma has given me leave to ask you whether you think it would look unsuitable or old for me to continue to wear short dresses for a year or two longer? I have been wearing them to come down to about two inches below my knees. I do so like the freedom that my short clothes give me that I do not like to give them up sooner than I can help. (We advise you to lengthen your dress gradually, having each new dress made two or three inches longer than the previous one. If you are very childish looking and petite you can wear dresses reaching the top of your boots up to 18 years of age.)

Englishwoman's Domestic Magazine, 1874

A change in shoe style also seems to mark maturity:

I completed my fourteenth year last August ... I do not mind wearing short frocks, but I do think I am too old to wear strap shoes ... I am a child I know, but I am not a baby, and can keep my shoes on my feet without ankle straps ... Do please, give me your opinion about my strap shoes – do other girls of my age wear them? Mamma will only let me have white stockings ... (Strap shoes are very pretty for young girls, and are fitted with pretty buckles for dress.)

Ibid.

The older school girl at the end of the period wore blouses and skirts with a quantity of underwear:

This is what a young lady wore, with whom I shared a room one night – beginning at the bottom, or scratch:
1. Thick, long-legged, long-sleeved woollen combinations. 2. Over them, white cotton combinations, with plenty of buttons and frills. 3. Very serious, bony, grey stays, with suspenders. 4. Black woollen stockings. 5. White cotton drawers, with buttons and frills. 6. White cotton 'petticoat bodice' with embroidery, buttons and frills. 7. Rather short, white flannel, petticoat. 8. Long alpaca petticoat, with a

flounce round the bottom. 9. Pink flannel blouse. 10. High, starched white, collar fastened on with studs. 11. Navy-blue tie. 12. Blue skirt touching the ground, and fastened tightly to the blouse with a safety-pin behind. 13. Leather belt very tight. 14. High button boots.

Gwen Raverat, *Period Piece*, 1952, writing of the 1890s.

Hairstyles

These are less helpful in distinguishing boys from girls than might be expected. Toddlers, irrespective of sex tend to have shoulder length hair, though boys rarely have a centre parting. In the late 1870s and 1880s, the fashion for cropping girls' hair can make them look very boyish.

After the age of 6 or 7 it is well to cut the hair short which permits a regular washing … and ensures coolness and health. There is much diversity of opinion … but the Americans who are quite famous for beautiful hair, are in the habit of cutting it short between the ages of 6 and 12 years. … After the age of 10 or 12, when the hair is permitted to grown long, it has been the fashion lately to allow it to hang down over the back for some years, or, indeed, until finally 'turned up' and our fair-haired baby developed into the more full-blown glories of young ladyhood.

The Queen, 1878

Family unity

This is often demonstrated by dressing brothers like one another, and sisters alike. Age is demonstrated by the variations in length of the trousers for the boys, and hem length for the girls. That such an outward demonstration of family unity was not resented is illustrated by its frequent persistance into adult life:

'Priscy', said Nancy, gently, as she fastened a coral necklace exactly like her own, round Priscilla's neck, which was very far from being like her own. 'I'm sure I'm willing to give way as far as is right, but who shouldn't dress alike if it isn't sisters? Would you have us go about looking as if we were no kin to one another … and I'd rather you'd choose, and let me wear what pleases you.'

George Eliot, *Silas Marner*, 1860. (Even though the novel is set a generation earlier, the sentiments seem more appropriate for the period in which it is written.)

Men's dress 1836–1900

The changes in men's clothes through these six decades are variations on a theme. The garments, coat and trousers, worn over shirt and waistcoat, change minimally in cut but significantly in their proportion throughout the period and these modifications are more easily observed from our longer perspective than they were within the period:

But, after all, the changes of fashion are not sufficiently rapid or violent in respect of men's dress, to make even our grandfathers uncomfortable on account of their peculiarity. If the hat brim and coat collar have lost what was once considered a graceful curl, if huge shirt collars and stiff cravats have given way to a freer arrangement for the neck, if blue swallow-tailed coats and brass buttons have been succeeded by blue frocks without them, and buff waistcoats with painfully tight appendices, by white waistcoats and the liberty of the leg, the change is not great enough to … make old men ridiculous even in our streets.

Habits of Good Society, circa 1860

Whatever the garment, the choice and its cut were determined by a man's desire to conform, to have:

respect to his profession and position in society.

Ibid.

For:

… in cities and populous communities. There appearance is inevitably the index of characters.

Etiquette for Gentlemen. 1866

The conventions were rigorously categorised:

To be 'undressed' is to be dressed for work and ordinary occupations, … To be 'dressed' … since by dress we show our respect for society at large … is to be clothed in garments which the said society pronounces as suitable to particular occasions.

Habits of Good Society, circa 1860

There was an abundance of advice on choice of garment:

[for] A well dressed man … there are four kinds of coat which he must have; a morning coat, a frock coat, a dress coat and an overcoat. An economical man may do well with four of the first and one each of the other per annum … The dress of an English Gentleman in the present day should not cost him more than a tenth part of his income on an average … a man with £300 a year should not devote more than £30 to his outward man. The seven coats in question will cost about £18. Six pairs of morning and one of evening trousers will cost £9. Four morning waist coats, and one for evening, make another £4 … Gloves, linen, hats, scarves and neckties, about £10, and the important item of boots at least £5 more … a sufficient wardrobe for a well dressed man who employs a moderate tailor.

Ibid.

With the competition of ready to wear, prices remained stable or even fell proportionately within the period:

The middle-class young man on £15 gets about four new suits a year … the smart man has a fresh coat for every day in the week. He will start the season with about twenty suits costing about five guineas each.

The Tailor and Cutter, 1890

Day clothes

The mood of day clothes of the 1840s and 1850s was tight and formal:

Today in compliment to his five more years, he was all in black and brown – a black satin cravat, a brown velvet waistcoat, a brown coat, some shades darker than the waistcoat, lined with velvet of its own shade and almost black trousers, one breast pin – a large pear-shaped pearl set in a little cup of diamonds – and only one fold of gold chain round his neck, tucked together right on the centre of his spacious breast with one magnificent turquoise.

> Jane Welsh Carlyle, *Letters*, 1845
> on receiving a visit from the Comte D'Orsay

But there was a slow yet increasing movement towards greater informality:

The best walking dress for non professional men is a suit of tweed of a uniform colour, ... gloves not too dark for the coat, a scarf with a pin in the winter, or a small tie of one colour in the summer, a respectable black hat and a cane ... But in London, where a man is supposed to make visits as well as lounge in the Park, the frock coat of very dark blue or black, or a black cloth cut-away, the white waistcoat, and lavender gloves, are almost indispensable ... The frock-coat ... should never be buttoned up.

> *Habits of Good Society*, circa 1860

We are rapidly degenerating into a slip-shod state of things. After a time Frock coats and even Morning Coats will be entirely a thing of the past ... Dress in our day has ceased to be the index of man's social position.

> *The Tailor and Cutter*, 1878

A reporter at Charing Cross noticed:

There were nearly two lounges to one Morning Coat and quite three lounges to one Frock Coat, the proportions per thousand working out as follows; Lounges 530, Morning Coats 320, and Frock Coats 150.

> *The Tailor and Cutter*, 1897

Evening clothes

For evening wear:

... black cloth trousers ... the strait-jacket ... the *habit de compagnie* ... the swallow tail ... Fortunately ... the tail-coat of today is looser and more easy than it was twenty years ago ... The only evening waistcoat for all purposes for man of taste is one of simple black cloth with the simplest possible buttons. These three items never vary for dinner party, muffin-worry or ball.

The only distinction allowed is in the necktie. For dinner opera and balls this must be white ... The black tie is only admitted for evening parties ... The shirt-front ... should be plain with unpretending small plaits ... The gloves must be white, not yellow.

> *Habits of Good Society*, circa 1860

Distinctions blurred:

The black neck tie is almost gone out; so that there is no scope for choice ... nor even in the matter of the shirt front ... as simple as possible relieved with small and unpretending studs.

> *Etiquette for Gentlemen*, 1866

... decided partiality for a white tie ... although subject to the disadvantage of being *de rigeur* among waiters ... always considered unexceptional.

> *How to Dress ...*, 1876

But these distinctions were reinstated with the introduction of a new garment, the dinner jacket, referred to in 1888 as the Dress Lounge or Tuxedo (US):

Semi-dress coat; a dress jacket, a popular three seamer, suitable for ordinary dinner, theatres and smoking concerts ... a little shaped to the figure, a roll collar faced with silk, two outside pockets, the edges do not meet. Same material as the dress suit.

> F. T. Prewett, *The West End System*, 1889

The cut modified within the period; it was tight and formal in the 1840s and 1850s when

Ease is now looked upon as the desideration in all articles of dress.

> *The Gazette of Fashion*, 1861

It changed again to become longer and closer fitting:

Frocks and all coats are long and the skirts flat.

> *West End Gazetter of Fashion*, circa 1876

The buttoning up mania is acute among the young men and the coats seem made to hide the collar itself.

> *The Tailor and Cutter*, 1878

In the 1890s, clothes are squarer cut with marked shoulder emphasis:

The shoulder seam well raised on the shoulder to give width and squareness to the shoulders.

> *The Tailor and Cutter*, 1895

Trousers balanced the line of the outfit:

The best cut trousers are always subject to a displacing of the seams and it is only with straps that they can be held in their proper position.

> *The Gentleman's Magazine of Fashion*, 1849

A greater number of variations were introduced; such as 'pantaloons'

Tight trousers buttoning on the ankle with 4 or 5 small buttons.

> *The Gentleman's Herald of Fashion*, 1854

Zouaves or Peg-tops as they are variously termed are decidely in great favour.

> *The Gentleman's Herald of Fashion*, 1859

Patterned trousers with checks and stripes were fashionable. Stripes at the seams were popular in the later 1850s and early 1860s:

Those stupid stripes down your trousers, what do they mean?

Punch, 1854

The line tightened in the later 1860s:

The fast young gents will be horsey and wear them tight to their legs [but] in the higher class trades trousers are made of the straight-up-and-down or military style, slightly defining the knee.

The Tailor and Cutter, 1869

There were variations such as those which flared at the ankle worn by:

... a few of the very fast school who are decidely horsey, more the style of a cad than of a gentleman.

West End Gallery of Fashion, 1870

Trousers were tighter again in the 1880s:

Modern trousers are close and small-bottomed and require narrow pointed boots.

The Gentleman's Magazine of Fashion, 1884

– and looser in the 1890s; when there was an innovation:

Trousers have not varied much in shape or material, but we all must have noticed the revival of the crease down the centre of the leg.

The Tailor and Cutter, 1895

A man shouldn't turn his trousers up unless there is mud out of doors, and he should take particular care to turn them down again before he enters a house ... You see, when you turn your trousers up you collect a lot of mud and dirt in the turned-up portion, and hostesses have a kind of prejudice against having large portions of mud brought into the house.

'The Major' of Today, *Clothes and the Man: Hints on the Wearing and Caring of Clothes*' 1900

Leisure and sports clothes

... a strict accuracy of sporting costume is no longer in good taste, [for] ... shooting and fishing ... An old coat with large pockets, gaiters in one case ... thick shoes ... a wide-awake ... make up a most respectable sportsman of the lesser kind.

Habits of Good Society, circa 1860

For picnics:

... great latitude of dress ... ladies ... in morning dresses and hats; the gentlemen in light coats, wide-awake hats, caps or straw hats ... morning dress of the sea side ...

For boating:

... white-flannel trousers, white rowing jersey and a straw hat. Pea jackets ... when their owners are not absolutely employed in rowing.

For cricket:

... you want nothing more unusual than flannel trousers, which should be quite plain, unless your club has adopted some coloured stripe thereon, a coloured flannel shirt of no very violent hue, the same-coloured cap, shoes with spike in them and a great coat.

Habits of Good Society, circa 1860

For lawn tennis:

This aristocratic and fashionable game ... opinion is equally divided between trousers and knickerbockers ...

The Gentleman's Magazine of Fashion, 1882

Flannel cricketing shirt, trousers with sash round the waist.

The Gentleman's Magazine of Fashion, 1886

The basic sports jackets and breeches of the second half of the century were the Norfolk jackets, introduced in the 1860s:

once popular and still not uncommon ... a quarter of a century ago, generally known as the Norfolk shirt ... pleats to give full play to the back in shooting and in exercise generally ... the belt keeping it close to the figure.

T. H. Holding, *Coats*, 1888

This was usually worn with knickerbockers, introduced in the 1860s as a looser form of breeches:

... originated with sportsmen, now worn by tourists for comfort and freedom. Not so full as on introduction. Buckle at the knee preferred to elastic ... either [they] are cut 3″ wider in the leg and 2″ longer than breeches; the knee band 1″ deep with a side buckle.

F. T. Prewett, *West End System*, 9th edition *circa* 1890

For riding:

... similar to that in which you walk, though what is called a jacket is more convenient than a frock coat. Do not ride in patent leather boots.

Etiquette for Gentlemen, 1866

For fox hunting:

For hunting ... cord breeches and some kind of boots are indispensable ... so too if you do not wear a hat, is the strong round cap ... and a scarf with a pin in is more convenient than a tie ... The red coat ... is only worn by regular members of a hunt ... you are better with an ordinary riding-coat of dark colour, though undoubtedly red is prettier in the field. If you *will* wear the latter, see that it is cut square, for the swallow tail is obsolete ... Again your 'cords' should be light.

Habits of Good Society, circa 1860

For bicycling the dress changed when the low safety bicycle was introduced, replacing the penny farthing in the 1880s:

The Bicycle dress is no longer the patrol jacket and

tight knee breeches, instead a Norfolk or Lounge Jacket and Knickerbockers.

The Tailor and Cutter, 1890

Sports and leisure dress at the end of the period:

On the river ... most men wear plain grey flannel coats and trousers ... white or tan shoes or boots ... A similar get-up will do for the mornings at the sea-side, or you can wear a knickerbocker suit. Don't wear a silk tie with tennis or boating flannels ... A white duck suit is a good suit to have at the sea-side. The man who is economical will make the same knickerbocker suit do for cycling, golfing and shooting. In this case the coat should be a Norfolk jacket ... with a pair of grey flannel trousers. The two together make a good knockabout suit to be used at places and on occasions when fashions don't matter.

The 'Major' of Today, *Clothes and the Man. Hints on the Wearing and Caring of Clothes*, 1900

Accessories

Jewellery was copious in the 1840s, thereafter restrained, though a tiepin and watch-chain with assorted pendants were features of the last quarter of the century.

Top hats are fashion items and alter in shape. Their history is best observed from the photographs themselves, but to summarise: during the 1840s they are tall and concave with the sides becoming straighter in the 1850s and tapering from crown to brim in the 1880s. They are lowest in the later 1860s and later 1890s.

Professional connotations as the mark of the doctor, the lawyer and the businessman:

Stockbrokers, merchants and others engaged in the city wear tall hats, both in their office as well as out, all day long as a matter of form, and almost of etiquette.

Ada S. Ballin, *op cit.*, 1885

Hard felt hats, more or less cylindrical in shape are worn for semi-formal towns and country occasions, usually with lounge suits. The 'bowler', with oval rounded crown, is introduced in the 1860s. In the 1870s, the felt hat with a crease in the crown, the Homburg, is introduced. For country and sporting wear, the broad-brimmed felt or straw 'wide-awake' is worn until during the last quarter of the century, when it is increasingly replaced by the rigid, narrow-brimmed boater.

Coiffure

During the 1840s hair was worn medium long and sometimes the sideboards extended into whiskers. A side parted slightly curly bob was popular for younger men, older ones preferred to perpetuate the styles of the Regency with the hair brushed from the crown straight to the front of the head and waved around the face.

1850s:

elegant young men who part their hair down the middle.

Punch, 1854

In the 1860s and 1870s hair was medium-long and side partings were usual, but during the 1880s hair was worn shorter. Centre partings were the mark of the 'masher', the ultra smart young man. During the 1890s, hairstyles were smooth and short.

... hair [avoid] turning it under in a roll, or allowing it to straggle ... or having it cropped.

How to Dress ..., 1876

Facial hair became fashionable during and after the Crimean War in the later 1850s and 1860s. Dundrearies, named from Lord Dundreary, the effete Heavy Swell in *Our American Cousin*, 1858 are extra long and exaggerated versions of the normal:

As to whiskers [they] should never be curled, nor pulled out to an absurd length. Still worse is to cut them close with the scissors. The moustache should be neat and not too large and such fopperies as curling the points thereof, or twisting them up to the fineness of needles – though patronized by the Emperor of the French – are decidedly a proof of vanity.

Habits of Good Society, circa 1860

Beards are optional until and during the 1860s:

It is not long since an Englishman with a beard was set down as an artist or a philosopher. In the present day literary men are much given to their growth.

Ibid.

Beard ... moderation.

How to Dress ..., 1876

Moustaches become increasingly popular from the 1870s and by the end of the century can be large and elaborately dressed.

Shaving was not uncomplicated and many men patronized barbers.

If not:

If we shave at all, we should do it thoroughly, and every morning ... The chief requirements are hot water, a large soft brush of badger hair, a good razor, soft soap that will not dry rapidly, and a steady hand ... If you can afford it you should have a case of seven razors, one for every day of the week, ... the use of violet-powder after shaving, now very common among well-dressed men, is one that should be avoided ... almost always visible, and gives an unnatural look to the face.

Habits of Good Society, circa 1860

Special groups

Garments could be combined and manipulated to suit their needs.

[A man] must avoid certain articles of attire which are either obsolete or peculiar to a class. Thus unless a man is really a groom, why should he aspire to look

like one? Why should he compress his lower limbs into the very tightest of garments, made for a man of seven feet high, and worn by one of five, necessitating in consequence a peculiar crinkling from the foot to the knee, which seems to find immense favour in the eyes of the stable-boy ... unless you are a prize fighter ... why should you patronize a neck-tie of Waterloo blue with white spots ... commonly known as the 'bird's-eye' pattern ... If your lot has not been cast behind the counter of a haberdasher, can there be any obvious reason why you should clothe your nether man in a stuff of the largest possible check ...?
... Or, if fortune did not select you for a 'light' in some sect, or at any rate for the position of a small tradesman, can you ... defend the fact that you are seen in the morning in a swallow-tail black cloth coat, and a black satin tie? ... It was at one time the fashion to affect a certain negligence which was called poetic, and supposed to be the result of genius. An ill-tied if not positively untied cravat was a sure sign of an unbridled imagination; and a waistcoat held together by one button only, as if the swelling soul in the wearer's bosom had burst all the rest. If in addition to this the hair was unbrushed and curly, you were certain of passing for a 'man of soul'.

Ibid.

Solicitors and doctors hardly ever wear frock coats; always morning coats.
The Gentleman's Magazine of Fashion, 1887

Countryfolk wear:

... smock frock and high lows (over-ankle boots)
Habits of Good Society, circa 1860

The carter, shepherd and a few of the older labourers still wore the traditional smock-frock topped by a round black felt hat, like those formerly worn by clergymen. But this old country style of dress was already out of date; most of the men wore suits of stiff dark brown corduroy, or, in summer corduroy trousers and an unbleached linen jacket known as a 'sloppy'.
Flora Thompson, *Lark Rise to Candleford*, 1954
writing of the 1880s and 1890s

Bibliography

The history of photography can be studied most readily and enjoyably in the permanent displays at the Science Museum and the Kodak Museum (now at the National Museum of Photography, Film and TV). There is an ever increasing number of books on the subject and good basic introductions to the history of the techniques are:

The Arts Council of Great Britain exhibition catalogue, *From Today Painting is Dead; the Beginnings of Photography* (1927)

Brian Coe, *The Birth of Photography* (1977)

Brian Coe, *George Eastman and the early photographers* (1973)

Brian Coe and Paul Gates, *Victorian Studio Photographers* (1975)

Brian Coe and Bevis Hillier, *The Snapshot Photograph* (1977)

Helmut and Alison Gernsheim, *The History of Photography* (1969)

Mark Haworth-Booth, *Old and Modern Masters of Photography* (1981)

Bernard Newhall, *The History of Photography* (1964)

D.B. Thomas, *The Science Museum Photography Collection* (1969)

There are exhibition catalogues and monographs on most of the main figures:

H.J.P. Arnold, *William Henry Fox Talbot* (1977)

The Arts Council of Great Britain exhibition catalogue, *Frank Meadows Sutcliffe 1853–1941, Photographer of Whitby* (1974)

R. Bartlett Haas, *Muybridge, Man in Motion* (1976)

Edinburgh, National Galleries of Scotland (Sara Stevenson) *David Octavius Hill and Robert Adamson, Catalogue of their Calotypes taken between 1843 and 1847 in the Collection of the Scottish National Portrait Gallery* (1981)

Helmut Gernsheim, *Lewis Carroll, Photographer* (1969)

C. Harvard (intro.), *Paul Martin, Victorian Snapshots,* (1939)

Peter Turner, *Peter Henry Emerson, Photographer* (1969)

The application of photography to the recording of personal and social life in the nineteenth century is dealt with in:

Gail Buckland, *Reality Recorded: early documentary photography* (1974)

H.J. Dyos and M. Wolff (eds.), *The Victorian City, Images and Reality* (section by G.H. Martin) (1973)

D. Francis, *The Camera's Eye,* (1973)

Michael Hiley, *Victorian Working Women* (1979)

Derek Hudson, *Munby, Man of Two Worlds* (1972)

O. Mathews, *Early Photographs and Early Photographers, a Survey in Dictionary Form* (1973)

W. Sansom, *Victorian Life in Photographs* (1974)

Gordon Winter, *A Country Camera* (1966)

There is also a series published by Batsford on Victorian and Edwardian history from old photographs.

Photographs are used among the sources for H. and A. Gernsheim's *Queen Victoria, a biography in word and picture* (1959) and *Edward VII and Queen Alexandra, a biography in word and picture* (1962). A. Gernsheim's *Fashion and Reality* (1963) uses photographs to illustrate a history of dress between 1840 and 1914. Aspects of related graphic sources can be compared by using: A. Bott, *Our Fathers, 1870–1900* (1932), and A. Bott and I. Clephane, *Our Mothers* (1932). The specific topic of fashion illustration will be found in M. Ginsburg, *An Introduction to Fashion Illustration* (1980), while the relationship of fashion plates to photography is examined in M. Ginsburg, *Fashions in Photographs* in Prof. Margaret Harker (ed.), *The European Society of the History of Photography Symposium* (1981).

The history of dress and fashion has an even more copious literature. Once again, museum displays are a good way to begin this study. J. Arnold, *A Handbook of Costume* (1974) can be used as a list for the collections but it is important to check its recommendations against a current list of museums and galleries as displays do alter, sometimes at short notice. Many museums publish short but useful introductions to Victorian dress.

The most accessible costume bibliography is that published by the Costume Society of Great Britain, and their journal *Costume* gives an annual review of current literature. Some basic books which will help with the dating of

historic and family photographs are:
R. Corson, *Fashions in Hair* (1965)
C.W. Cunnington, *Englishwomen's Clothing in the 19th century* (1937/41)
C.W. and P. Cunnington, *Handbook of English Costume in England in the 19th century* (1970),
P. Cunnington and C. Lucas, *Occupational Costume in England from the 11th Century to 1914* (1967)
E. Ewing, *History of Children's Costume* (1977)
C.H. Gibbs-Smith, *The Fashionable Lady in the 19th century* (1974)
A. Mansfield and P. Cunnington, *Recreational and Sporting Costume* (1969),

S. Newton, *Health, Art and Reason: Dress Reformers of the 19th Century* (1974)
The history of dress accessories is dealt with in a Batsford series:
June Swann, *Costume Accessories 1: Shoes* (1982)
Vanda Foster, *Costume Accessories 2: Bags and Purses* (1982)
Fiona Clark, *Costume Accessories 3: Hats* (1982)
Valerie Cumming, *Costume Accessories 4: Gloves* (1982)
Hélène Alexander, *Costume Accessories 5: Fans* (1983)

Index

Figures in **bold type** refer to photograph numbers